Table of Contents

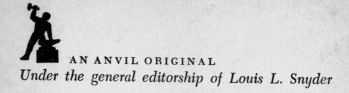

AN ANVIL ORIGINAL
Under the general editorship of Louis L. Snyder

THE MODERN
AMERICAN CITY

CHRISTOPHER TUNNARD
Professor of City Planning, Yale University

D. VAN NOSTRAND COMPANY, INC.
PRINCETON, NEW JERSEY
TORONTO · MELBOURNE · LONDON

TO MY WIFE

VAN NOSTRAND REGIONAL OFFICES
New York, Chicago, San Francisco

D. VAN NOSTRAND COMPANY, LTD., *London*
D. VAN NOSTRAND COMPANY (Canada), LTD., *Toronto*
D. VAN NOSTRAND AUSTRALIA PTY. LTD., *Melbourne*

COPYRIGHT, 1968, BY
CHRISTOPHER TUNNARD
Published simultaneously in Canada by
D. VAN NOSTRAND COMPANY (Canada), LTD.

PRINTED IN THE UNITED STATES OF AMERICA

Preface

What aspect of the American City could be more "modern" than its recent historiography? Current attempts to chronicle its development represent a new area of exploration, one that is only beginning to be accepted as a field for research and thus is about to enter the university and college curricula in those forward-looking academic institutions which recognize its importance.

The author's interest in the dynamics of the American city began in London in 1938, when he first opened a copy of Lewis Mumford's *The Culture of Cities*. Many of the interpretations in the following pages differ from those in that seminal work. They are the result of subsequent years of acquaintance with American art and architecture, with its city planning, technology, and socio-economic life, during which time the author had formed his own opinions of cities in the United States. One of the tasks has been to underline the importance of certain key figures and movements, such as the architect Richard Morris Hunt and his school, the banker Charles Dyer Norton, the City Beautiful planners and certain major reformers whose contributions have been neglected in recent urban literature, yet which are part of the mainstream of American urban achievement.

Acknowledgments are made to Wayne Andrews, Alan Burnham, Iris Buten, Alexander Garvin, C. McKim Norton, Harry J. Wexler and Harold Wise for their help in providing information for the text. Some of the earlier readings were assembled by Henry H. Reed, Jr. and the author during the preparation of a previous book, *American Skyline: The Growth and Form of our Cities and Towns*. Able assistance on marshalling the remainder was given by Steven Douglas. Thanks are also due to Earl Collier for preparation of the index and to Mary Triffin for the typescript.

CHRISTOPHER TUNNARD

Part I

THE MODERN AMERICAN CITY

CHAPTER 1

The Modern American City

A National Institution. The modern American city appears after the Civil War. It has seen many changes since then, but they have been absorbed in a structural fabric that has only begun to alter radically in our own generation.

The dominating characteristic of the post-Civil War city was its emergence as a national rather than a sectional institution. "In the generation following the Civil War the city took supreme command," observed Arthur M. Schlesinger, pioneer chronicler of the American city from 1878 to 1898. The development of the West and the growth of industry everywhere established this supremacy, together with national systems of transportation and verbal communication.

Reflecting a national concern, Americans are now asking: How accurately does the city reflect the aims and goals of the United States? How does it differ *sui generis?* and from other cities of the world? What are its prospects and chances for survival?

A way of shedding light on these questions is to examine what has been achieved, what men have tried (and often failed) to do in cities, and how the city is changing in our own time. With the United States facing a doubling of its population in the next fifty years, such an examination assumes great urgency if the citizens are to be properly informed on a major issue of the day. It is important, too, to discover how attitudes to the city have changed: How does the nation regard its cities and towns? Are they the proud standard bearers of our civilization, or stepchildren, waifs of the political system, doomed to receive only crumbs from the family table? Are there traditions, governmental and otherwise, which encourage or inhibit the continued good health of the civic body? Is there a national policy or course of action to be taken on the city and its physical development, as UNESCO has recommended, that every country should establish? These and other questions concerned with the dynamics of the American city are being asked increasingly.

Defining the City. For an institution so complex, probably no one definition will suffice. Former attempts, such as:
"Regardless of type or configuration, the city is a changeable
but continuing society, largely made up of households or family
groups, its geographical area being restricted by comparison with
the population it contains," [1] may still be valid, but do not always
give us the flavor and excitement that many cities generate. The
very notion of a city is eclectic; and a sociologist, a psychiatrist,
an architect, and a city planner would all have their own ideas
of what a city is and ought to be. Rather than attempting a
definition here, it is more important to note a few factors that
should be taken into account in making one. (*See Reading
No. 1.*)

First, the city is not a single environment, but a range of en-
vironments. There is a great difference between a city of 50,000
people and a super-metropolis of five million. Similarly, there
are differentiations within a city; there are people living in it
whose paths may never cross; one neighborhood is not like
another. In a large city there are a multitude of overlapping
jurisdictions. And every functional component of a city has its
own zone of influence—the schools, the factories that encourage
cross-town journeys to work, or the theaters that may draw their
audiences from the whole city and beyond.

It follows that while it may be possible to characterize a city
in space, as the Bureau of the Census does with its "urbanized
areas," to describe the city as a social phenomenon may be much
more difficult. Indeed, the ideas here remain as numerous as
those engaged in urban studies. Robert Park was the first to put
forward an ecological theory of the city, suggesting that it was
a "cultural area" with laws of its own. Immigrant or racial
colonies, he thought, tend to follow these laws and maintain
themselves within the larger urban area. Ernest W. Burgess divided the cities into a series of concentric urban rings, starting
from the central business district and working out to the commuters' zone. Sub-communities were classified by Louis Wirth
in his famous book, *The Ghetto;* and since his day studies of city
problems—juvenile delinquency, low-income housing, and the
like—have multiplied. Social-psychological theories, having

[1] Christopher Tunnard, *The City of Man* (New York and London,
1953), p. 8.

much less relation to physical surroundings than Park's ecological approach, have recently concentrated on forms of social action and orientation. There have been economic theories as well, from Marx and Engels to Pirenne and Dickinson. Even the art historians have taken up studies of the city as an artifact, the consensus being that it must be broken down into component parts to be analyzed qualitatively.

Behavioral scientists are discovering that the city is losing much of its old formal structure and at the same time gaining dominance, noting that the traditional linkage—City-Suburb-Countryside—makes less sense than before. The city is losing its long-cherished political autonomy, also. (*See Chapter 7.*) All these factors and more must be taken into account in asking, "What is a city?"; and the controlling idea that both spatial and social characteristics are rapidly changing must be accepted.

Myths and Social Attitudes. A phenomenon of the magnitude of the city produces a body of lore which colors the attitudes of men toward what they have created. North American myths are as strong as those of any other part of the world, and often linger generations after the conditions that gave rise to them have disappeared. One of these is the earliest: that the Puritan city was an experiment of moral worth, filled with a population of "visible saints" and cemented with neighborly love, an example to the succeeding plantations, but especially to decadent Europe, of the heavenly city on earth. When, after 1691, a new charter made property rather than piety a condition for freemanship in the Massachusetts Bay Colony, an important belief was lost. But it was remembered, and has been contrasted ever since with the goals of the marketplace in the successive stages of capitalism that have developed here. The American city has thus always been a place where things ought to be better than they are. The City on a Hill is still the vision, but conditions are not right for improvement. In 1890 the immigrants were blamed; one-fifth of the urban population then was foreign-born. Today, the influx of southern Negroes into northern cities overshadows problems common to black and white that could be solved away from the heat of controversy. The philosopher Santayana found that in America cooperation was everywhere accepted, but he did not live long enough to see the present social plight of the cities; his colleague Charles Sanders Peirce, writing in 1871, found on the contrary a tremendous question mark in the rampant individualism that marked his age and lingers into our own, causing him to wonder "whether men really have anything in common, so that the *community* is to be considered as an end in itself." Peirce thought that the relative value of the two factors, individual and community, raised the most fundamental practical question of the day and that every person and public institution "that we have it in our power to influence" should be made aware of the possible conflict of goals. The concept of the common good is never very far away from the American urban mind, a condition that should not seem strange even in the light of much violent and irrational urban history. After all, both religious and nonsectarian groups have sought to build the ideal or communal city in all periods of American life.

No amount of city-boosting, speculation, false optimism, crime, graft, or greed can obscure the myth that Americans mean their cities to be good, with the image of those tiny communities clinging like limpets to the shore of Massachusetts Bay fixed firmly in the national mind.

There is also the myth of the American West, which is related to the Puritan ideal because the West was first made holy, a new Eden, in the American ethos, and then secularized in the idea of progress and empire.

"Time's noblest offspring is the last," wrote Bishop Berkeley, promising the end of all corrupt imperialisms and the establishment in America of a greater Power. Everyone was astonished by the way cities sprang up in the forests, like some kind of miracle, although Alexis de Tocqueville noted in his diary sagely enough that it was the roads, the canals, and the mails that made it all possible. "In a new State," he wrote in 1831, "one of the first things done is to have the mail come. In the Michigan forests there is not a cabin so isolated . . . that it does not receive letters and newspapers at least once a week; we saw it ourselves." And although to the Frenchman a place like Cincinnati was "a city which seems to want to rise too quickly for people to have any system or plan about it," others were filled with astonishment at the "style and magnificence of its buildings." By 1830, says the urban historian Richard C. Wade, the rise of the cities was one of the dominant facts of Western life.

Thus the development of cities became linked with the idea

of progress, and progress itself still carried a sacred aura. And when ideas of progress are mingled with holiness and national pride, it is easy to see why de Tocqueville found it impossible to draw from Americans "the least truth unfavorable to their country." He found that most of them boasted about their surroundings in a way that was disagreeable to strangers and that there was much of the small town in their attitudes. These attitudes were carried to extremes and institutionalized in the second half of the nineteenth century with the rise of civic booster groups and real estate associations. The planning of Oklahoma City in 1890, known as "The City Built in A Hundred Days," is a notorious example. Cultural facilities it had none of; and six real estate offices, the Board of Trade, and the California Barber Shop and Bath House seem to have been all that this metropolis could offer to the world. George Babbitt's attitude to his real estate business as well as to his city is typical of this hubris carried over into our own century, and involves little exaggeration on the part of his creator, Sinclair Lewis.

When things go wrong in cities, as they do in economic depressions or in the struggle for civil rights, common attitudes of despair, horror, or inertia are not especially to be wondered at in the light of apocalyptic visions once held and ideas of material progress firmly ingrained.

What Is "American" about the City?   Apart from the strong relationship between American ideals like that of religious liberty and the building of communities by various sects, there was no deliberate attempt to be different—the people who came to these shores built much as they had in their former homes. The New England farmhouse had clapboards outside instead of cobb (a mixture of clay and chopped straw) as in England, because the weather was more inclement here; but they still used oak beams and planks until the beginning of the nineteenth century. They copied Christopher Wren's churches in London and put them on town greens or commons. Later, when they were prosperous, they built in brick, as in Philadelphia, which on the eve of the Revolution was the largest city after London in the British world. They adopted the avenue and the boulevard in imitation of nineteenth-century Paris when Napoleon III was setting the fashion, and the apartment house from Europe when the cities were becoming crowded for lack of space.

In a sense, almost everything that was built in the cities became American. Just as the Renaissance architects who thought they were copying the ancients produced buildings the like of which were never seen before, a Christopher Wren church built in wood instead of brick or stone has become a unique national artifact. It must be said here, too, that in the architecture of sects like the Shakers, the balloon-frame house, and the skyscraper tower, American builders can claim originality as well as adaptive skill. It is also fruitful to explore trends of common usage within the country as well as to trace stylistic derivation, since in the cities the marketplace, class, and caste play important roles, with differences occurring as much in social or economic adaptation as in the more visible evidences of history.

The City as a Market. The modern American city has been called the business community *par excellence,* although it is to be noted that the European businessman gives his counterpart here a close race and frequently teaches him a thing or two. It is important to remember, however, that the cities have fulfilled their role as centers of trade and finance from earliest times and that they have increased their hold on commerce even in today's apparent decentralization. Certain it is that they were in command even when frontier life was strongest and that the Boston or Philadelphia banker had a large part to play in its expansion. Except for the Virginia planters, who disliked towns and forced Charles II to veto an act which would have established towns as tobacco shipment centers, the early settlers were charged with the rapid development of trade and reminded of "the great necessity, usefulness and advantages of cohabitation." The London Company sent instructions with its colonial bands to lay out wide streets, line up their houses in rows, and attend to their protection. Made independent and resourceful by hardship, the settlers gradually forged the agricultural market town, improvising with the open lot, the picket fence, and useful devices learned from the Indians. Seaports existed from the beginning. As mercantile capitalism merged into the period of industrial capitalism, cities of row houses, hotels, fine stone warehouses, government buildings, atheneums, and theaters began to appear; and the state capitols raised their domes, the national Capitol in Washington pointing the way.

But even with the growth of some amenities in the city, the

dominance of an urban business mentality became stronger. "At the bottom of all that an American does, is money; beneath every word, money." Although he might be generous, wrote an observer in 1834, it is not enthusiasm or passion that opens his purse strings, but policy, views of utility, or considerations of propriety that move him. Private interests became identified with the public good; it became fashionable to talk about making money, which was raised to the position of a virtue, and extolled in the pulpit.

This was no chance development in American life. Given the freedoms that existed, the immigrations of the poor and persecuted from Europe, the absence of an aristocracy, and the chances that everyone took in establishing a life in a new country, it was inevitable that men turned to money-making; with the growth of population, too, there was money to be made out of the expansion of the city itself. John Jacob Astor died worth twenty million dollars, made largely in New York City real estate; and nobody forgot that he had been a poor immigrant boy when he arrived. The incentive to make money applied to all, and the national slogan of "Bigger and Better" could be thought of for cities as well as every other aspect of life.

Although the "get rich quick" approach to urban life now applies to fewer groups than formerly, it helps to explain certain phenomena that differentiate the cities from those elsewhere. Business failures, which accompany the restless, moving instinct of the small speculator, account for empty stores, "bad" blocks, and the drearier commercial districts which sprinkle old and new cities alike. The importance of the hotel, often the first building in town, with its barroom the place in which business is transacted and its proprietor the most important citizen, is known to the world through Western movies. The lack of adequate public transit, in the early days only provided if a traction ring could reap the spoils, is another feature of a society which still considers that any enterprise that pays is best, public or private.

On the other hand, from the private sector have come many good things that have marked American cities in a special way. The great city art collections, symbolized best by the National Gallery in Washington, which was given by the wealthy Andrew Mellon and is maintained by the government; the public libraries given by Andrew Carnegie; and the work of great private foundations in building hospitals, centers for the performing arts, and so on . . . all these are to be found in greater profusion in America than might be expected. The businessmen's clubs and organizations should be mentioned also as agents for charity and good works in the American city. If the cities still lack many of the services that the countries of northwestern Europe consider to be a public right, it is because organizations like the American Medical Association, which are devoted to the preservation of private enterprise in their own sector of society, have played on a theme which is so familiar as to seem sacred. Like the hymn tunes of old, the strains of manifest destiny, holy purposes, and the accumulation of wealth linger in the minds of many Americans long after the conditions which inspired them have disappeared.

CHAPTER 2

A City Built Foursquare

The Ideal Plan.   Although public works have from early times been an important part of the economy, it will be seen from the above that a *national policy* toward cities has not been part of American intent. Constitutionally, the cities were made creatures of their states, which limited their borrowing powers and their legislative freedom. Internally, the cities differed considerably in the way they were governed, and differed from each other in early industrial specialization . . . brass towns, coal towns, railroad towns . . . which gave each a special character, or at least the stamp of a special class. A New England mill town has similarities with a southern cotton-spinning town, but bears little relation visually or socially to a resort city or a state capital.

The cities were mostly built by private enterprise, although a state legislature might provide funds or the national government make land grants, especially in the case of railroad towns.

The streets and parks were public; but generally speaking the municipal governments were not encouraged to own, buy, or hold land that could be bought and sold privately. Just as local government is the wayward child of American politics, the cities themselves were allowed to grow capriciously. Latterly, under the police power and the taxing power, certain local controls like zoning and graduated assessment act as a brake on wild speculation; but it can also be said that zoning has often been used to improve real estate values rather than to achieve the orderly growth of a community. (*See Chapter 6.*)

Yet with all the differences that isolation, uncertainty, and an often turbulent history produced, there was one national characteristic of cities making for an almost standardized product. This was the right-angled or orthogonal plan.

There is something recognizable and persistent in American use of the gridiron plan, which was employed from the very beginning in Anglo-America. The little mercantile towns were built on grids, exceptions like New Amsterdam (now the lower part of Manhattan), Boston, and Annapolis being rare. Later, Thomas Jefferson thought that the grid was the best method of laying out a city, and it was he who enshrined it in the national settlement pattern by the Land Ordinance of 1785. (*See Reading No. 2.*)

The grid has been called the hallmark of secondary, or colonial, settlement—a notion arising from the practice of the ancient Greeks in founding colonies, where it was very often used, while mother cities like Athens remained irregular, which Aristotle had advised was better for repelling invaders. This rather misses the point, which is that the grid had always been a favorite of trading societies, from the caravan cities of Asia Minor to the towns of the London Company in Northern Ireland, which Anthony N. B. Garvan suspects were the models for early towns in New England. The grid was eminently suitable to the trading groups of the Atlantic shore; and there is a long history of its employment by the early settlers, who were quite familiar with the laying-out of fields and "long lots" in rectangular form, as well as their market towns. The Nine Squares of New Haven, Connecticut, which tradition holds were laid out by the surveyor John Brockett in 1638, are an example of a town preplanned in this manner. Grants to the colonies mention rectangular plans, as do township grants and official instructions to governors. Independent-minded settlers did not always follow these instructions; so that, in practice, during the early period, rectangular layout occurs only in the boundaries of some of the colonies, in the ground plans of some cities and town centers, and in the division of common lands.

In those early days, the lining-up or contiguity of township lines was a minor concern of the settlers and only in the eighteenth century did colonial governments begin to insist on it. Tiers and blocks of rectangular townships five and six miles square began to appear in Maine, Vermont, the Pennsylvania frontier, and parts of New York. Except for the fact that it was traditional in North Carolina, the subdivision of these townships into sections of 640 acres, which later became the standard, cannot be found in colonial practice. Some authorities think that the "Frontier Stations" in Tennessee, which were often of 640 acres, may have been the prototype.

Jefferson's Influence. Whatever the precedents may have been, when the former eastern colonies began struggling over western land claims, the new nation decided to create more states, and they were as regular as could be. Jefferson was a member of the committee that in 1784 first set forth the system of rectangular surveys. The novelty lay in using parallels and meridians fanning to the cardinal points of the compass. That this precept was not always followed in practice is understandable in a sparsely settled wilderness.

Jefferson was quite thoroughly committed to the principle of rectangularity; and he liked checkerboards for towns as well, in one or two instances, when he was acting as designer, suggesting that alternate blocks in a town be left in green space as a public health measure. As chairman of the rectangular-survey committee, however, with his influence he modified the states' edges when they were bounded by rivers, making an irregular border on at least one side. Otherwise, the country was divided into regular sections, which in turn could be subdivided into half- and quarter-sections. Jefferson's proposed names for the areas thus defined were not adopted; if they had been, many Americans would now be living in states called "Sylvania" (for the territory near the Lake of the Woods), "Cheronesus" (the peninsula formed by the Great Lakes) or "Metropotamia" (for the territory containing the sources of seven large rivers).

Thus the settlement pattern of regions and nation ordained the shape of cities not yet born.

Within the town sections, regular as checkerboards or grids, little rivers and sometimes old post roads were the only break in the pattern. Later, railroads and, today, urban freeways introduced arbitrary curves and tangents; but apart from these everything was regular. Even the village green or courthouse square was missing, unless Eastern settlers from New England or Virginia had brought it with them. Some of the new railroad towns had plazas, but often the center of town was just a four-corners where two streets met. There were variations in the width of these, and sometimes alleys ran through the center of a block, as in the Back Bay in Boston—a planned development on filled land laid out in the 1850's, which has a sophisticated hierarchy of streets leading to Commonwealth Avenue, a once-fashionable tree-centered avenue and promenade.

Sometimes, when the town was laid out on one side of a river, the grid was "refracted": that is, in order to keep one set of streets at right angles to the stream (or lakeshore), separate grids had to be introduced as the bank changed direction. Minneapolis was planned in this way and still presents problems to the modern planner where the grids separate at angles, causing awkward traffic patterns and odd-shaped blocks. Refraction can also occur wherever land-jobbing, speculation, or municipal platting have dictated additions to an earlier plan.

Adaptable to land sale and transfer, the grid could be laid out by rudimentary surveying methods. As a ground plan for towns, it recommended itself to land-sharks and religious groups alike. (*See Reading No. 3.*) Had it not been mentioned in the Bible? "For the form of Babylon, the first city, was square, and so shall also be the last, according to the description of the Holy City in the Apocalypse." Most important of all, like the decimal money system proposed by Jefferson for the nation at about the same time, a settlement and township pattern based on a simple ratio, with townships one mile on a side, was easily understood by a people far separated in space and communication. Jefferson the statesman was aware of this

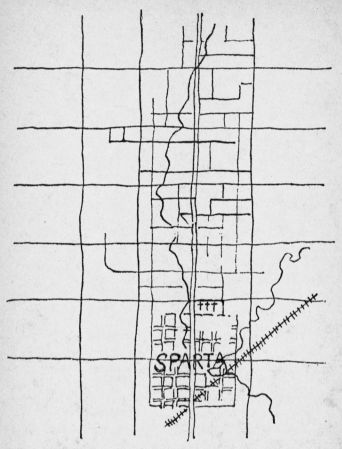

Fig. 1. THE NATIONAL GRID. *After the enactment of the Land Ordinance of 1785, the western states were disposed of in sections of 640 acres, which included townships. This is part of Monroe County, Wisconsin, in 1860, showing the town of Sparta as platted. Note how the main street of the gridiron town follows the section line and how neatly the hierarchy of lots, streets, and section lines mesh into an orthogonal settlement pattern, broken only by the river and the railroad line. (After* The Wisconsin Domesday Book, *Vol. 1, p. 133.)*

and counted it a useful factor in the orderly development of the Union. Thus the rectangular system of land division, modified by theorists like himself at the time of the founding of the Republic, became the prime element of town-building that can fairly be termed the result of national policy.

City and Metropolis. Jefferson was well aware that there were much greater questions than the one of what form the cities should take on the ground. He did not think they should be large, as indeed few were in his day. (Even as late as 1850 less than 13 percent of the population lived in cities, with only nine containing more than 50,000 people.) But if he had influenced the nation in favor of the gridiron plan, his advice was forgotten in the nineteenth century's proclivity for bigger and better and more of everything. The city of New York reached a population of one million by 1880, a figure Chicago proudly matched ten years later. "I view great cities as pestilential to the morals, the health and the liberties of man," he wrote, remembering the condition of the urban poor he had seen in Europe. Jefferson, who understood what Eli Whitney was doing in introducing exchangeable parts in gun manufacturing, nevertheless reckoned without the Industrial Revolution, which, although it began among the fields in the form of water-powered mills, soon found that a city-based labor force and cheap wages were essential to the new economy that was being created. The idea of the New Jerusalem was thenceforth only pursued as an objective which could immediately be achieved by sects and outsiders; and the new cities, built foursquare as they were, nonetheless came to match Manchester and Sheffield and Liverpool as sinkholes of filth and poverty.

After the Civil War, when the modern American city appears, the pace of development quickens, until in 1950 60 percent of the population lived in cities. Only three times—in the 1870's, the late 1880's and early 1890's, and the 1930's, each decade marked by an economic depression—does the pace slow down. Repelled and fascinated at the same time, Americans *en masse* show no signs of abandoning the city for some unknown new institution as yet uninvented. They have determined, as always in their history, to correct what they find in the new urbanized surroundings and to approximate as best they can on earth their forefathers' City on a Hill.

CHAPTER 3

The Picturesque City

One architect of genius they had . . . Richardson. I had the pleasure to know him: he is dead, alas!—MATTHEW ARNOLD[1]

The modern American city came into being with a great deal of lumber in its attic. Jefferson's neo-classic architecture, which he, like the first Napoleon, favored to make cities more beautiful, had been succeeded by a series of romantic revivals, of which the Greek temple style became by far the most popular in both North and South, where it was used not only for churches but for houses, banks, public buildings, and the great mansions of the antebellum planters. By 1860 it did not seem incongruous to build a Lombardic Gothic city hall (a style much favored by the English critic John Ruskin) next to a Greek Revival hotel or an Egyptian jail.

After the Civil War, all these evidences of art run headlong into a new age of technology and business, changing their form and character. (*See Reading No. 4.*) Exhaustion with the styles does not set in until the 1890's, when the public turns to a calmer, less nervous architecture of classical derivation and which in turn embellishes the cities with new building forms of startling magnificence (*vide,* the recently demolished Pennsylvania Station in New York, a *chef-d'oeuvre* of the architectural firm of McKim, Mead, and White, giants of the classical revival).

Technology. If the birth of the modern American city took place in an age of architectural revivals, its technology was new and spectacular. By 1861 railroads had reached out from the East, which was well-supplied, as far as Minnesota. The completion of the Union-Central Pacific across the continent in 1869 was a symbol of national pride, and the transcontinental roads that followed scattered towns and cities in ribbons through every state. The Civil War itself made cities; the importance of Pitts-

[1] *Civilization in the United States*

burgh and its iron foundries dates from this time. With men lacking to till the fields, the manufacture of farm machinery was begun in Chicago. The Overland Telegraph Company had spanned the continent before the War, and by the time war broke out an express service had done the same. These advances in communication changed the nature of some cities: flour-milling moved out to Minneapolis; meat-packing left Cincinnati for Chicago—which city, with the introduction of the refrigerator car in the 1870's became "hog butcher to the world."

Practical changes in the city itself came more slowly. Gothic and Greek revivals might battle for favors from businessmen, but mud was still the surface of most streets. Asphalt was widely used in Paris and London long before New York gave up its stone and wooden blocks. (*See Reading No. 5.*) Asphalt was laid in Washington streets in 1878, setting the pace for other cities. In that same year New Haven opened the first telephone switchboard; and two years later eighty-five other cities had done the same, with 35,000 miles of wire festooned above their streets. In 1873 the cable cars were in San Francisco; in 1878 the 6th Avenue elevated was built in New York; and in 1887-1888 the first electric trolley was seen in Richmond, appearing in fifty-one other cities by 1890. Boston built one-and-one-half miles of subway between 1895 and 1897; New York's system followed in 1904. By this time the wires were going underground, too, the telephone and electric-light lines forming their own complicated patterns among water, gas, and sewer mains. The first power plant had been built in 1882 on Pearl Street in New York; between 1883 and 1913 electricity had spread all over the city. (*See Reading No. 6.*)

Personalized transportation on rubber tires was not available in the first decades of the modern city, except in the form of the bicycle, which brought with it demands for smoothly paved streets. Mass transit, however, in the shape of the horse car, the cable car, and later the trolley, which became interurban, was essential to urban development. None whose job was in or around the city could afford to live very far from a line. This was the "classical" period of the modern metropolis, when central city, suburb, and farm land were still clearly defined, mass production and mass distribution not yet having arrived on a scale large enough to disperse the urban community very widely. (*See Reading No. 7.*)

The Taste of the People.   National taste was anything but classical, as we have seen. While it leaned to the French in the first part of this period and copied the Second Empire, there was no telling what foreign influence would crop up next, so great were the numbers of immigrants—Germans, Irish, and Swedish at first, followed by Mediterranean, Central European, and finally Oriental peoples—who brought with them customs that have become a part of American life. James Bryce, author of *The American Commonwealth,* found that the German immigration had promoted an interest in outdoor life, increased the taste for music, and introduced the less strict Continental Sunday. But he noted that most of those who came were of the "humbler" classes, scarcely influenced by their own literature, whereas trends in fashion were set by the foreign upper classes. The immigrants came to work in the mills, on the roads, and on the farms. Susan Fenimore Cooper's memoir of 1883 contains a glimpse of families trooping along the Boston Post Road at Mamaroneck, where her family lived—men, women, and children, hungry, dusty, and weary. Her grandmother gave them milk and biscuits, discovering they had just landed from a ship a day or two before. After a rest they went on their way to some distant manufacturing town. Anyone who has read of the Irish potato famine must wonder that these deprived people were able to bring as much as they did to enrich the national culture.

The mill towns they came to in the early days were those of the Boston Associates and their like at Lowell and Manchester—the first company towns. Later, with the development of the extractive industries of the West, mining and gold-rush towns appeared. Railroad towns were used by the owners to develop business for the lines. There were even "irrigation" towns in California . . . Redlands, Riverside, Pasadena, and Pomona . . . settlements which had found a practical way of sharing the cost of bringing water. Josiah Royce, the American philosopher who was brought up in the rugged California mining town of Grass Valley, notes the cooperation that circumstances force wherever men gather "in a few ragged huts." As the mineral gave out or was no longer in demand, cooperation and community faded away, some of the communities only to be revived as "ghost towns" for tourists in recent years. The violence and hardship of a copper-mining town like Butte, Montana, probably had to be experienced to be believed. When today's quiet and comfortable Americans are accused by Europeans of accepting violence as a means of settling disputes, they may or may not remember that this trait does not lie very far back in American history. "The wildness of that time passed into the blood of the people, and has left them more tolerant of violent deeds," Lord Bryce observed of the mining fraternity. But, like Royce and Santayana, he noted the "eagerness to run and help" that marked these little communities as it had the first frontier. The reality of the West had clashed with the myth of the West, but it was the image of "community" which made life possible on the edge of nowhere.

Back East, the newcomers had brought with them a taste for music; and a New York Symphony was founded in 1878. This was followed by the Boston Symphony in 1881, and Chicago founded one ten years later. German and Italian influence had much to do with the establishment of opera on a firm basis in New York by 1883. In that city the Episcopal Church provided reading rooms, gymnasia, and social clubs for the new citizens; but the social church was not confined to one denomination—we read that the Baptist Temple in Philadelphia and the Congregational People's Temple in Denver provided similar facilities in the 1880's.

The Cult of the Picturesque. Behind all the seeming fragmentation of taste lay a controlling idea to which the whole age subscribed, albeit without much awareness—the fashion for the picturesque. When the leading architectural critic Montgomery Schuyler writing in 1894 admired Vaux and Withers' Jefferson Market Courthouse in Greenwich Village (1872) (now being restored as a branch library) and Peter B. Wight's Academy of Design (1862), done under the influence of Ruskin in a Gothic manner, he was exhibiting in his own predilections the tenacious quality of this idea. (*See Reading No. 8.*) Indeed, it persists into our own day, and has become a controlling factor in modern taste. (*See Chapter 7.*)

To understand this influence on American taste in the first years of the modern city, it is necessary to know how nature was regarded in the nineteenth century. Having become somehow tamer, she could be looked at on equal terms: one could thrill to the wild landscapes of a Thomas Cole or a Bierstadt without fear of the wilderness, and Emerson's "gliding train of cars" took him through the most majestic scenery in the utmost comfort of red plush and perfect service. This new way of looking at nature had begun a century before in the doctrines of French Jesuit theorists like the Abbé Laugier in Paris and in the new English method of laying out large estates. It is hard to imagine today that the Abbé Laugier was introducing a revolutionary idea when in his *Essai sur l'Architecture* (1753) he applied picturesque principles to town planning. In walking through the town, he advised, one should never see the same sights, but should find each quarter new and different, "with a kind of irrgularity and chaos that suits great towns so well." He was rebelling against the strict regularity of the German city of Manheim's checkerboard plan and other Cartesian applications of the gridiron in the France of his day.

The English thoroughly agreed, although few John Bulls had ever heard of the Jesuit priest. They were busy laying out their gardens in the new landscape style. "Nature abhors a straight line," they had been told, so they tore up all the old formal gardens (something not easily done with towns), substituting curving shrubberies, clumps of trees casually placed in the middle and far distance, and artificial lakes elongated to look like rivers. One should never see the same sight twice in walking round the estate, says Mr. Milestone, a caricature of the English landscape gardener Humphrey Repton in Thomas Love Peacock's *Headlong Hall*. "Pray, what happens when you go round the garden for the second time?" interjects the long-suffering Squire Headlong.

The fundamental change in attitudes of the eighteenth- and early nineteenth-century tastemakers to nature was to look at a landscape differently—as a series of compositions which would appeal to a painter. Hence the term "picturesque."

There were other strains in the picturesque syndrome, developing somewhat later. But one of them, *rationalism*, was also prescribed by the French abbé, when he advocated the theory that the fixed principles of art can only be found in reason. This was taken up a century later by another Frenchman, Viollet-le-Duc, the great restorer of Carcassonne, Pierrefonds, and other monuments. His taste was for the Gothic, with which he clothed his architecture, since in that style "every part seemed necessary to the whole." His writings espoused the notion that the logic of the plan, the structure, and the materials dictated the design, turning architecture into a kind of pseudo-science. Although his most important work was done in the first part of the Second Empire, his interest to us is his influence on American post-Civil War architects like Hunt, Richardson, and Sullivan, whose famous phrase "form follows function" sums up the rationalist approach.

The Cult in the United States.   The fashion for the picturesque had reached epic proportions when the American nation was ready to resume the postwar round of everyday life. True, the earlier romantic phase of architecture had run its simpler course: the Greek Revival, a romantic style *par excellence,* had left the East for the South and West; few architects still favored the Egyptian even for the brutal penitentiaries on the cities' outskirts. (Although it had once been in vogue for cemetery gates, the association of the Egyptian style with a "pagan" religion invited critics to denounce it as "an architecture of embalmed cats and deified crocodiles.") Cast iron had come in; and Henry Van Brunt, a follower of Viollet-le-Duc, urged American architects to use it "with honest regard for its nature, attributes and capacities." That they were slow to do so is evidenced by the fact that as far back as 1848 James Bogardus had built the first all cast-iron building in New York, but few architects had followed his lead. Their rich patrons, beginning to come with the rise of the financier, were not particularly interested in structural method.

Lombardic or Venetian Gothic was "in," as evidenced by the popularity of the aforementioned Jefferson Market Courthouse and the work of Furness and Hewitt in Philadelphia, who built the Pennsylvania Academy of Fine Arts and the offices of the Provident Life and Trust Company, both in the 1870's, albeit ignoring some of the "honesty" of Gothic construction. There was also the Mansardic Style (the mansard roof was favored during the Second Empire), which was as much used for country villas at Newport and in the early suburbs as it was in towns. The brownstones, which could be built singly but came to spread out row after row in cities like New York, owed more to the London town house than to Paris; but the first apartment houses or French Flats derived from prototypes in the latter capital, as the name implies. (Built in 1869, the first recorded American apartment house, the Stuyvesant in New York City, was designed by Richard Morris Hunt, who became the Vanderbilts' architect, as Frederick Law Olmsted became their landscape architect.

Washington, D.C., a city which has often followed the French mode, received its chief example of Second Empire architecture in 1871, next to the White House. Designed by A. B. Mullet, the many-storied building which formerly housed the Department of State now contains the Executive Offices of the President.

Hunt and Richardson. If there was as yet no national policy for the growth of cities, neither was there any attempt to regulate business and industry, which were essential ingredients of that growth. The truth was that they were becoming engrossed by a few financial geniuses, who, while they did not control the proliferation of thousands of new enterprises, nevertheless set the tone for the entire country in financial matters. John Pierrepont Morgan, Andrew Carnegie, and John D. Rockefeller, all born within a few years of each other in the late 1830's and each with his special talents in banking, industrial development, and corporate enterprise, became the chief figures of the early days of the modern city. Old Commodore Cornelius Vanderbilt (1794-1877) had shown them what could be done with a railroad empire; and although railroads remained the chief items of speculation through the Great Depression, as the period of the 1870's and 1880's came to be called, new manufactures in steel and new ways of doing business gained enormous wealth for these financial leaders, even while lesser business brains were gambling and losing more modest fortunes.

It was a grandson of the old Commodore, William K. Vanderbilt, who built the first really sumptuous private house in America on the corner of Fifth Avenue and 52nd Street. Now demolished, it rose between 1879 and 1881. Richard Morris Hunt was its architect, the first American to be trained at the Paris École des Beaux-Arts. This was no Second Empire pastiche, but a return to the French Renaissance of an earlier day; and it was to be an inspiration for later architects like McKim, Mead, and White, who were to lead America toward a more classical vision of its cities. Beside this exemplar to the increasingly important architectural profession, Hunt led the nation away from a provincial taste. He was the experimenter, and all the rest were to follow. (*See Reading No. 9.*)

By contrast, Henry Hobson Richardson evolved an intensely personal architecture. From the 1870's to 1890 he and his followers enjoyed an extraordinary vogue. His style, which is now known as Richardsonian Romanesque, marks the culmination of the first phase of the picturesque movement in architecture, which is taken up again in our own century by Frank Lloyd Wright. Indeed, Richardson's interest in materials, his insistence on the architect's attending to all the decorative details, his asymmetrical compositions, and his use of the round-headed arch, all forecast the younger man's work. John La Farge, who did the murals for Richardson's Trinity Church in Boston (1876), thought him a genius. He records how Richardson reluctantly came under the spell of Viollet-le-Duc as a Paris student, after having joined the militants who hissed the great restorer away from his lectures. (They were objecting to the medievalist's insistence on French Gothic as a model.) And in fact Richardson relied less on Viollet-le-Duc than did Hunt, who spent happy days with the restorer at Pierrefonds, where he was rebuilding the castle for the Emperor's son. Richardson called Trinity Church, his first big commission, "a free rendering of the French Romanesque." By going back to the architecture of the so-called Dark Ages in Europe, he introduced a novelty, at the same time bringing a fortress-like character to libraries, jails, banks, and domestic buildings by his use of massive stonework and circular towers.

Impressive in girth and character as well as in his designs (Louis Sullivan was an admirer), Richardson won over his millionaire clients. While he never equalled Hunt's success in gaining sponsors like the Vanderbilts, he built a store for Marshall Field in Chicago and almost a whole town for the wealthy Ames brothers at North Easton, Massachusetts. He was well-educated and drew intellectuals as clients as well as businessmen. Henry Adams was one, although the house Richardson designed for him opposite the White House is no longer standing. The adjoining house, also built by Richardson for John Hay, had rich interiors, with heavy beamed and decorated ceilings, extensive wall paneling, and Turkish carpets on the floors. It was nevertheless "quiet, dignified and welcoming" according to the twentieth-century architectual critic Talbot Hamlin.

There is no question that Richardson by the very force of his

architectural style belongs among the greatest of American architects. He and his disciples, among whom can be counted the Boston firm of Shepley, Rutan, and Coolidge, left their mark on the
cities. The libraries, universities, and other public buildings can
be identified by the massive random stone bases as well as the
use of terracotta. When Richardson's Pittsburgh Courthouse and
Jail was scheduled for demolition recently, hundreds of admirers
signed petitions to save it. These buildings lend a special flavor
to the modern American city, but like the battlemented armories
that began to appear in the strife-torn America of the 1870's,
they must find new uses in order to survive in our own day.

"A Sense of Enlarged Freedom." Nineteenth-century attitudes to nature presumably can best be understood by the way
nineteenth-century man manipulated natural forms. By the 1860's
they had arrived at a thoroughly picturesque esthetic in laying
out the new suburbs, the country estate, and the central park.
Frederick Law Olmsted, the inventor of the term "landscape architecture," had a hand in all of these developments, and remains
the chief innovator of the time in park and city planning.

Born in 1822, Olmsted early showed a love for nature and
farming. He recorded in his diary that as a boy he sat at the
feet of a "poor scholar" who read and translated Virgil to him;
it is easy to suppose that in some of the lectures he later attended
at Yale he learned more of that Latin author and the story of
his preserving the farmland near his birthplace, "from where the
hills begin to stoop, sloping their ridge to the water and the ancient beeches." Significantly, many of Olmsted's park compositions have the bucolic atmosphere of the Augustan poet's images.

In any case, he turned landscape architecture away from the
wildly romantic phase in which Edgar Allan Poe, the poet, and
Andrew Jackson Downing, the landscape gardener, had wreathed
it. (*See Reading No. 10.*) Downing died at thirty-seven, leaving
an English partner, Calvert Vaux, who joined with Olmsted. Together they won the competition for the new Central Park in
New York in 1858, the design being more naturalistic than other
entries, one of which essayed a large map of the world done in
flowers. Olmsted and Vaux used the contours of the land to advantage, introducing quantities of American shrubs and trees as
well as many of the popular ornamentals of the day. Vaux was

the architect of the team, but there is no doubt that Olmsted was interested in design; two books he put into the hands of his apprentice pupils were Sir Uvedale Price on the picturesque and Gilpin on forest scenery. "You are to read these seriously," he told them, "as a student of law would read Blackstone."

A few years later the partners were laying out Prospect Park in Brooklyn, which Olmsted preferred to the design of their more famous Central Park. The Long Meadow is certainly Virgillian in feeling, in spite of all the vicissitudes it has since undergone; and it is encouraging that today local groups are anxious to restore Prospect Park, not to some World's Fair playground, but to what the designers thought it should represent.

Recent attempts by historians to make Olmsted into a nineteenth-century Universal Man are based largely on his well-known interest in social conditions. In their report on Prospect Park of 1866, the team gives its reasons for laying out a park in the first place. They asked themselves this question: "Is there any pleasure which all persons can find at all times in every park? And, if so, what does that pleasure depend on?" (*See Reading No. 11.*)

Their answer is worth quoting and the italics are theirs:

> The answer unquestionably must be . . . that there is such a pleasure, common, constant and universal to all parks, and that it results from the feeling of relief experienced by those entering them, on escaping from the cramped, confined and controlling circumstances of the streets of the town; in other words, *a sense of enlarged freedom* is to all, at all times, the most certain and the most valuable gratification afforded by a park. The scenery which favors this gratification is, therefore, more desirable to be secured than any other, and the various topographical conditions and circumstances of a site thus, in reality, become important very much in the proportion by which they give the means of increasing the general impression of undefined limit.[2]

Another basis for park planning, the designers thought, was to provide means for the relaxation of tensions. In that pre-Freudian period they called it "the unbending of the faculties." "We find this impossible," they went on, "except by the occupation of the imagination with objects and reflections of a far dif-

---

[2] Olmsted, Vaux and Co., *Report of the Landscape Architects* (Brooklyn, 1866), p. 13.

ferent character from those which are associated with their 'bent'
condition." Hence scenes of repose, interesting plant compositions, boating on the lake. They spoke too of "the recuperation
of force" that a laborer would gain from a day in the open air.
Conditions were wretched in most Brooklyn factories and en-
forceable public health measures still in the future. (The first
state Board of Health was established in Massachusetts in 1869.)

All these considerations led the two men to emphasize the pastoral element. This, they said, consisted of combinations of trees,
standing singly or in groups and casting their shadows over broad
stretches of turf "or repeating their beauty by reflection upon
the calm surface of pools." Such scenery is in the highest degree
tranquilizing, they maintained, quoting the Hebrew poet: "He
maketh me to lie down in green pastures; He leadeth me beside
the still waters." They formed a tranquil lake below the Long
Meadow, subordinating everything to this one theme. Evocative
compositions of a minor nature were included: there was "a slight
approach to the mystery, variety and richness of tropical scenery . . . gay with flowers and intricate and mazy with vines and
creepers, ferns, rushes and broad-leaved plants." Stony ravines
would remind the visitor of mountain scenery.

In the smoky, noisy city of the 1860's and 1870's, already cut
through with lumbering steam trains over which hung jerry-built
tenements, the movement for new parks was a godsend. Olmsted,
after his early demonstrations in New York and his famous
speech "Public Parks and the Enlargement of Towns," persuaded
dozens of communities all over North America from Montreal
to San Francisco to undertake this form of civic improvement.
(*See Reading No. 12.*)

The Parkway and the Picturesque Suburb. In the same
report to the Commissioners of Prospect Park in Brooklyn appears Olmsted and Vaux's pioneering plan for a parkway. This
early example should not be confused with the parkway as we
know it today, on which abutting property owners have no right
of access. In the days of the private carriage, the firm's design
included sites for villas along the edge of the new facility, which
was to form an approach to the park. Modeled on "the Avenue
of the Empress" in Paris (now the Avenue Foch), it had a central mall divided into two parts to make room for a middle road-

way for pleasure riding and driving, the ordinary paved traffic roadways with their sidewalks remaining outside the mall for commercial vehicles, pedestrians, and access to the houses. The space from house to house was to be 160 feet. With extensions to Coney Island, Fort Hamilton, and Ravenswood, the designers suggested, spacious and healthful accommodations for a population of 500,000 could be made within a ten-minute walk of the parkway system. Part of this was actually built and is today known as Ocean Parkway.

Thus Olmsted and Vaux entered the field of city planning, Olmsted continuing in it long after the partnership was dissolved in 1872. In 1857 Vaux had written in his *Villas and Cottages,* "The great charm of natural landscape lies in its well-balanced irregularity. This is also the secret of success in every picturesque village." In 1868 the firm laid out a picturesque village themselves, nine miles out from the business center of Chicago; it was called Riverside. After a slow start it became a success as a "suburban village" accessible to businessmen by rail from the city. The streets are curved, as Olmsted put it, "to relieve the dull and flat monotony of the prairie"; and he introduced a central park along the Des Plaines River.

This was an opportunity to introduce picturesque street planning on new ground, since in the existing cities the gridiron was too well entrenched. Olmsted was able to experiment with the new street layout for Charles Eliot Norton on land he owned in Cambridge, Massachusetts, between his own house and the University; but otherwise he was confined mostly to the growing suburbias such as Tarrytown Heights (1872) and Roland Park, Baltimore (1890).

In other hands, suburbs were not usually so carefully planned. In 1882 the Real Estate Record and Builders' Guide noted only three "suburban parks" as they called them: Llewellyn Park, a New Jersey development of the 1850's, with romantic villas by Alexander Jackson Davis; Menlo Park, San Francisco; and Riverside itself. The Guide referred its readers to the success of Bedford Park outside London, pointing out that there were a hundred localities within fourteen miles of New York's City Hall where well-planned and serviced suburban villages could be built. The first suburb in the modern sense of the term (planned by a developer for commuters) had been Brooklyn Heights, which advertised a sale of lots in 1819. It was accessible to Manhattan by the new steam ferry; the owner, a New York merchant, H. B. Pierrepont, used the gridiron plan and even the 25 by 100 foot lot plan adopted by the neighboring city in 1811 and known as the Commissioners' Plan for Manhattan. This was the strait-jacket Olmsted and his successors tried to loosen as the modern American suburb emerged.

A Waning Movement. In the 1870's Olmsted became a friend of H. H. Richardson and landscaped the grounds of libraries and railroad stations that the corpulent architect received as commissions. But the now-famous landscape architect counted as his most important private commission the grounds and arboretum of Biltmore, the George W. Vanderbilt mansion near Ashville, North Carolina. In 1886 he had planted the surroundings of the Vanderbilt family tomb on Staten Island and "advised a Vanderbilt colony" at Lenox, Massachusetts. The mausoleum was by Richard Morris Hunt, and the landscape architect was to be associated with him at the Chicago World's Fair, where Olmsted did the ground plan; at Biltmore, where again Hunt was the architect, and in the grounds of which the aging Olmsted was painted by John Singer Sargent in 1895. Biltmore was Olmsted's last work before his capacities failed.

By this date, however, a profound change had come over the public taste in architecture; it was only in landscape architecture and park planning, carried on by Olmsted's son and a growing number of landscape architects, that the picturesque movement lingered. Even at its height it had not influenced the layout of the city proper, as we have seen. In fact the choicest examples of urbanism that can be pointed to in the post-Civil War period show little evidence of the picturesque beyond their architecture. Outstanding among these was the Back Bay in Boston, between the Public Gardens and Fenway Park (laid out by Olmsted in 1879-1881). Its planner was the architect Arthur Delevan Gilman, who introduced a promenade down the center of a fine new avenue (Commonwealth Avenue) and designed the Arlington Street Church (Unitarian) in brownstone in 1859. Later, on the avenue, H. H. Richardson built a Romanesque church, employing the sculptor Bartholdi (designer of the Statue of Liberty) to adorn the frieze with trumpeting angels.[3] But the urbane character of the residential streets, which were strictly regulated as to height and setback, using the typical Boston house plan in most cases, is the antithesis of picturesque irregularity, pointing to the fact that Americans retained a traditional interest in urban taste of the Federal Period. In fact, they only had to look up from the Back Bay to Beacon Hill and the State House by Charles Bulfinch to see what that tradition was; happily, in our own day, this earlier model of urban design is preserved for us by the creation in 1955 of the Beacon Hill Historic District.

Perhaps the spirit of the first years of the modern city is symbolized best by the Brooklyn Bridge, which signaled the rapid advance of technology yet was clothed in Gothic arches. As much admired today as it was on its completion in 1883, it proves that a nation on the move did not entirely ignore the spiritual nourishment that only art can provide.

[3] The architects of the picturesque era were unfortunate in not having squares to set off their buildings. Commodore Vanderbilt's purchase of what was left of Hudson Square, a formerly handsome residential compound, from Trinity Church, New York, in 1866 to build a railroad freight yard is symbolic of the age. Richardson's Back Bay Trinity Church faced on what almost became a picturesque square, in an architectural sense. A triangle formed by three streets, to Copley Square, was added in 1876, the Ruskinian Gothic first home of the Museum of Fine Arts, and in 1887 the Romanesque S. S. Pierce building, both now demolished. Boston is still trying to make a "square" out of this irregular space. (See: Walter M. Whitehill, *Boston: A Topographical History,* Cambridge, Mass., 1959.)

CHAPTER 4

The City Beautiful, 1880-1893

Nature is picturesque, but what man creates should be beautiful, or else it is inferior—WILLIAM DEAN HOWELLS[1]

When Richard Morris Hunt visited the Centennial Commission's International Exhibition in Philadelphia in 1876 he looked carefully at many things. Foremost, in that most picturesque of all World's Fairs, he observed that the architecture of the American exhibitors was wanting in anything like monumental grandeur. "As compared with the exhibits of other nations," he remarked, "one is struck with the ambitious pretensions of our designs, overloaded as they so often are with meretricious ornament." These buildings tried, he thought, to produce a novelty of effect, which resulted in a lack of harmony and repose, so essential to "good work."

The Centennial also caused Hunt to think of municipal improvement. He noted that municipalities were paying more attention to "the sanitary science," the lighting of streets with gas, telegraphic communication, and rapid transit. He urged them to follow Baron Haussmann of Paris in opening boulevards, "giving breathing space to populations of millions." In America, where so much remained to be accomplished, he found many city officials loath to undertake modern improvements that he thought were necessary because of the rapid growth of large cities and manufacturing towns. This was an early call for city planning on a scale commensurate with the need.

Most interesting of all, he chastised the organizers of the Fair for ignoring "the amelioration of dwellings for the laboring and industrial classes," citing the Improved Industrial Dwelling Company of London, with a capital of £1,000,000, which had housed 10,000 persons by 1876, and the medal that the French Emperor had received in the Paris Exhibition of 1867 for his efforts in the same direction. As if in answer to Hunt's criticism, the Im-

[1] "Letters of an Altrurian Traveller," *The Cosmopolitan,* XVI, December 1893, p. 231.

proved Dwellings Association heeded this early plea for better housing with two projects, one in Brooklyn and one in Manhattan, between 1878 and 1880; but in general the efforts made in this direction were disappointing, and early laws to combat slums, beginning with New York's in 1865, had very little effect.

Hunt spanned two worlds. Starting under the spell of Viollet-le-Duc's rationalism he emerged in later life as an advocate of the classic spirit in architecture. He lived to see the birth of the city-planning movement in America. As an advocate of housing for the working class, he was far ahead of his time; and as a founder of the American Institute of Architects he imbued in younger men a sense of duty to society which welded them into a profession. "Architecture as it has been in the United States," wrote a critic in 1909, "may be said to have begun with Richard Morris Hunt." (*See Reading No. 14.*)

Growing Pains.   The city had become not only a consumer, building up elaborate credit systems and paying for improvements over long periods of time; but it provided new ways of doing business, with its franchises that gave monopolies to traction kings and suppliers of all kinds of services. Municipal politics deteriorated, and were prodded in turn by reformers, authors, statesmen, and publicists. No one knew how to govern a big city. They were plagued by fires, which caused damage in the many millions each year, and by strikes. (One reason for the large number of armories in the city was to provide a means for controlling strikes and riots.) Bryce told Americans in the 1880's that city government was the most conspicuous failure of their political life. Under such criticisms, cities began to abandon their former loose administrative patterns and set up mayor-and-council governing bodies, in order to fix responsibility. But the party machines grew stronger in an age of graft and quick profits; and "good government" campaigns, although they shed light, were not often given the opportunity to do so from public office. The reformers' turn had not yet come. They remained outside, with the social church, the slum mission, and the burgeoning trade unions. "Efficiency," in the forms of commission systems of local government and "city management," did not appear until the early years of the twentieth century.

By present-day measurements all this seems like a storm in a teacup. The city of 1880 was limited in size, bound by primitive transportation systems. New York City, with its present budget exceeding five billion dollars, seems overwhelmingly fraught with problems by comparison. Yet in the beginning years of the modern city there were problems that fortunately have disappeared. It was as late as the 1870's that the germ theory of disease was conclusively proved, and it was only during the next two decades that cattle and pigs were forced out of public streets. Manure yards stood next to swill milk plants and dirty public markets, all these occupying space in residential districts. Privies overflowed into basements; and the Metropolitan Board of Health in New York City, established in 1866 in advance of a threatened cholera epidemic brought by immigrants from Europe, was set up with standards too low to combat careless sanitation habits. Even hotels had privies in their back yards. New York's 25 by 100 foot lot proved a strait jacket when single-family houses became tenements or new tenements were built; and when in 1879 an amended Tenement House Law was adopted, this same lot saw the prize-winning dumb-bell multiple dwelling squeezed onto it. The dumb-bell tenement made use of an air shaft for outside lighting of rooms, but ignored the reality that twenty-four families could not live decently in a six-story building with no yard. Yet so slow was the progress of housing reform that the dumb-bell tenement remained the "model" until 1901. (*See Reading No. 15.*)

To the growing urban middle class, not yet freed by technology to escape to the suburbs, the ex-farm laborers and mixed-nationality immigrants who occupied the crowded slums were a people apart, conflicting in a nightmarish way with the American dream of a classless society. When, as late as 1911, the Fifth Avenue Association was formed, this was largely to prevent garment-workers from being seen on the Avenue, with the movement of the industry uptown. It was not until the 1920's, when the advertising campaigns for body deodorants had their effect on large numbers of people, that New Yorkers stopped complaining about the odor of humanity in the subways.

Yet the growing city was an exciting place. It was "the place to be"; and although they may not have realized it, the middle classes were accomplishing more in the way of reforms than they had ever dreamed of a few years before. New problems caused by the cities rubbed off on national movements; and it was in the cities that free schools, public libraries, women's property rights, and prison reform had their stimulus. The National Conference of Social Work had its genesis in the National Conference of Charities and Correction, to which Victorian-sounding body the Massachusetts Inspector of Charities spoke in 1881 on "Insanity in the United States," his Ohio counterpart having spoken the year before on "The Apathy of the Churches." Social questions were being aired, and new institutions formed to deal with urban situations. The "river wards" of Chicago (those less fortunate communities housing Germans, Bohemians, and Poles after the Civil War) needed such an institution; with their language problems the new residents could not demand proper services from either landlord or municipal government. They lacked control over their American-born children, and culturally the river wards assumed a "backwoods" aspect that industriousness alone could not redeem. This was the milieu in which the settlement house was born; it gave direct evidence that a bilateral community existed, since its personnel was drawn from residential districts only a few blocks away. The river wards created the philanthropic community, of which Jane Addams was a representative. Her settlement house and three others in Chicago were more aggressive than the churches in helping the poor to help themselves; and until the universities superseded the settlement house as a social research institution and public welfare became more common, they played an important role in American civic affairs. Staffed largely by women, they continued an American tradition of female activity in education and cultural advance in a country that, until recently, had forced its male population toward gainful occupation in the mill or counting-house; even the wealthiest members were "decorously draped in the garment of strenuous endeavor," as the Chicago novelist Henry B. Fuller put it. They did not have to work, but knew it was important to keep up the appearance of doing so.

Building Tall. The prosperous citizenry of the bilateral community of Chicago segregated themselves first by moving westward, and in later years to the near South and North Sides, where they lived along the new boulevards and in the suburbs of Lake View and Hyde Park. No industrial worker set foot here, and it was only in the heart of the city that all classes mingled together. The South Side had good suburban railroad service into the business district; east of State Street was the South park system. In 1880, Woodlawn, which has figured in the news so prominently since the advent of urban renewal, was a country village; but it was beginning to build stores and commuters' homes. The lake cities were now growing more quickly than the river towns; and after the railroads came to Chicago she easily outstripped St. Louis, Cincinnati, and New Orleans, which were supported mainly by river commerce.

Chicago itself was cut up by the surveyors' section lines. A mile apart, they formed the through streets; and on them secondary business centers started up, with shops, taverns, and blacksmiths' forges becoming located along the way. In the 1920's, these section and half-section line streets were to be zoned for business, thus fixing a pattern long established. But the central business district was then comparatively small—the Chicago River defined it—and this led to a practice often remarked on by foreign observers: building replacement. Homer Hoyt, whose book *One Hundred Years of Land Values in the City of Chicago* is a classic of its kind, remarks that there were probably few spots in the downtown district in 1933 that had not been occupied by at least three, if not four, sets of buildings. Recent unsuccessful attempts to save the Garrick Theater and the Courthouse show that this process continues. With it is tied up the story of the tall building.

Before 1880 there were very few buildings higher than six stories and none higher than eight. Chicago was behind New York in this, since Hunt's Tribune Building appeared in 1873. It was partly iron-framed, as if attempting to carry out Viollet-lè-Duc's prophecy that an architect would appear who would one day erect a vast edifice whose frame should be entirely in iron. But there was a new metal now, steel cheapened by the Bessemer process; and skeleton construction could become a reality.

There was a business logic behind the introduction of the steel frame. The now-very-old-fashioned "business block" of brick or masonry could be seen in every city and small town, sometimes with a higher central portion with the date or name of the owner in raised lettering. With pressure to lift the height of buildings, and as the power sources for the elevator improved, these masonry supporting walls had to be thickened to take the added weight. This reduced valuable ground floor shopping and banking space, although one could lease the top floor at a premium, as in the ten-story, 230-foot high Western Union building, serviced by elevator, built by G. B. Post in 1873-75. Grain elevators with iron frames and brick curtain walls had been built in Brooklyn and Philadelphia in the 1860's. But in Chicago, in 1883, an engineer, William Le Baron Jenney, commissioned to design the ten-story Home Insurance Building, used wrought iron for the first six floors and Bessemer steel beams for the top floors. This was a breakthrough; and although Jenney's buildings are plain to the point of dullness, architects soon took up the challenge, and the Chicago School of Architecture was born. Men like Holabird and Roche, Daniel Burnham, and John Wellborn Root built tall business blocks of architectural distinction; while Louis Henri Sullivan added a decorative system of ornament based on plant forms, with more than a hint of reference to Viollet-le-Duc. In the Wainwright Building in St. Louis, Sullivan claimed that the steel frame was first given authentic expression; but critics have differed, one of them pointing out that in this building the columns are all alike yet every other one contains a steel core, that the frieze and cornice are out of all proportion to the columns on which they rest, and all are absolutely at variance with the movement within the frame.

Architectural considerations aside, by 1890 the new buildings had pressed up to thirteen stories, and department-store owners in Chicago had discovered that people would sooner ride the elevators than walk a block along the street to another store. Very soon all land in the center of the city was revalued on the basis of what it would return if occupied by sixteen-story buildings. Yet the tall blocks exercised a fascination which could not be explained by economic considerations of net income alone. "Shapes of Democracy" Walt Whitman called them, and tenants poured out of the obsolete six-story buildings into the new and modern quarters, with their large expanses of glass and airy elevator cages. One could eat, drink, get a haircut, and have his office all in the same structure. Manufacturing concerns set up offices there—a new trend—and the promoters of the coming Chicago World's Fair sought the prestige of locating in the "cloudscrapers," as they were called in their first years. (*See Reading No. 16.*)

Actually, the American city had to wait for its famous central silhouette until the second wave of "building tall" swept the country after the turn of the century. Adler and Sullivan, with great difficulty, had raised a seventeen-story tower on the side of the Auditorium Building, which was so heavy as to require special weighting in order to settle evenly. The "envelope" had been raised, but a church spire could still command attention in the bursting city of the 1880's and 1890's.

Truly, the big city seemed to have come of age by 1880. If farm land was being taken up in increasing amounts and agricultural land-booming was common ("Kansas became a vast insane asylum covering 80,000 square miles," one state official commented), the city too had its booms, based partly on new forms of transportation. The elevated steam train pushed New York's land boom, beginning in 1879-1880. Its usurpation of city streets furnished "a unique example of civic prostitution of appearances to utility. It possessed that Caliban quality, cheapness," commented the Real Estate Record and Builders' Guide in 1894, by which time the elevated system had spread into Brooklyn and the Bronx, extending over open fields and attracting investment. On Manhattan the boom on the Upper East Side north of 96th Street lasted until 1884, after which time the West Side was recognized as the great speculative area. The most important change downtown was the conversion of a slummy residential district between Washington Square and Canal Street into the warehouse and loft district that we know today. That New York was now a big city was confirmed by the United States Census of 1880, which announced a population of over a million people. It also had great wealth and enormous individual fortunes, which the display of mansions springing up on Fifth Avenue underlined.

Yet the city retained a provincial aspect; the air of a great metropolis was missing. The architecture of the 1870's was everywhere. There were a few apartment houses—one, The Bradley, being built as far uptown as 59th Street, between 5th and 6th avenues. The breaking up of the big city estates, many of which dated from colonial times, like the Dyckman property, had not produced any interesting new building. With the contract system large tracts of land could be secured, usually on a ninety-day contract, by depositing 5 percent of the purchase money. The building-loan operator was very active, contributing not a little to the gigantic inflation and flimsy enterprises that preceded the panic of 1873. The entire section east of Chatham Street, the Bowery, and 3rd Avenue was already destined to become the chief tenement district of the city, with immigrants who did not venture farther settling there by the thousand. The middle class lived in interminable rows of brownstones, with the high stoops which marked the New York town house, "all of them devoid of architectural style and beauty," as a contemporary remarked. (*See Readings Nos. 17 and 18.*)

The Resurgence of the Classical. In spite of all this mediocrity, and perhaps partly because of it, by 1880 the discerning eye could have seen that future urban architecture would take an entirely different course. America was beginning to discover its own past.

In architecture, the American past was no inconsequential matter. There was the Baroque period of the late eighteenth century, when splendid churches and town houses had graced the seaport towns. There was Jefferson's introduction of a Roman style, typified by his Virginia State Capitol at Richmond, as well as a host of such neo-classic architects as Charles Bullfinch who raised the domed State Capitol in Boston and Robert Mills who designed the Treasury building in Washington. Mills had been succeeded as architect to the government by Ammi B. Young, who designed post offices and customs houses in cities all over the country, one of which, a handsome columned building of cast-iron construction in Galveston, Texas, has recently been restored by the General Services Administration. Washington itself had a Baroque plan, designed by the Frenchman Pierre Charles L'Enfant; and it had the United States Capitol, which was being completed and decorated in the classical manner all through the Picturesque Era. There was the Washington Monument, completed after thirty years by 1884. There had been urbane residential squares, now vanishing in the path of the industrializing city, but a few remaining to point the way. Louisburg Square in Boston, Jackson Square in New Orleans, and Washington Square in New York were fine remaining examples. Everywhere could be found traces of the classical past. New Yorkers had only to look at their own City Hall, then being dwarfed by the first tall buildings, to discover a beautifully-proportioned exterior begun in 1803, with distinguished interior detailing, a curving staircase of marble in the rotunda, a ring of graceful columns, delicate iron tracery, and other features that had equaled the best work being done in the Europe of its day. For contemporary work in the classical manner, New Yorkers could see the Wil-

Fig. 2. THE CONTINUING CLASSICAL TRADITION. *Jefferson City, Missouri. The second capitol building (above), on a bluff over-looking the Missouri River, by the architect A. Stephen Hills, was com-pleted about 1845. The present capitol, dedicated in 1924, continues the Roman motif. (After Herman J. Meyer, Universorum.)*

liamsburg Savings Bank, built in 1875 by George Browne Post, a pupil of Richard Morris Hunt. An impressive structure with grouped pilasters and a dome, it graced the city of brownstone and brick which made up the Brooklyn of that time.

At the height of Richardson's fame, when he was designing Trinity Church, another group met in Boston to save the Old South Meeting House, where—in its heyday—bitter tea had been brewed for King George III. It says something for James Russell Lowell, President Eliot of Harvard, and other distinguished Bostonians, that although their taste was more inclined toward buildings like the Ruskinian Gothic Memorial Hall in Cambridge by Van Brunt, they banded together to save a building (for which there was already a purchaser ready to pay $400,000) in the growing business district of Boston. "The Old South Meeting House was the best thing our fathers could do in their day,"

Lowell reminded his friends, "and they thought it beautiful." Actually, Old South is one of the finest churches of the eighteenth century, with a very beautiful spire which is a refinement on the church tower developed by Christopher Wren. Lowell's group was successful; and he would have been pleased indeed to know that his own house in Cambridge, a fine Federal period mansion, has been left in our own time by the widow of the art historian Kingsley Porter to be preserved forever by Harvard University.

Men of taste (which in this case meant knowledge of the world of art) could now be counted on to take an interest in urban surroundings. It should be remembered that most of them had town houses, unlike the present situation in which people of leisure have escaped from the problems of city life. Many more were to be built in the coming years, the spirit of rivalry which the Vanderbilts had encouraged with the building of their Fifth Avenue mansions becoming in men of lesser fortunes an ostentatious striving to build in limestone or marble a dwelling for entertainment and modest display. If they used brick now, it would be for Georgian or early Colonial revival buildings as soon as news of the rediscovery of these American styles had been spread in the country by the new architectural firm of McKim, Mead, and White. These observant designers had taken a trip through New England in 1877, just after McKim had come back from the École des Beaux-Arts in Paris, where his architectural training had taught him to appreciate the value not only of the French Renaissance, but of all the classical past. Years later, when the classical manner of building had been accepted, McKim wrote to a student in Paris: "When you come home ready to build, you will find opportunities awaiting you that no other country has offered in modern times. The scale is Roman and it will have to be sustained."

CHAPTER 5

The City Beautiful, 1893-1910

Reintroduction of Roman Scale. "It requires long and fine training to design on classic lines," the Director of Works of the World's Columbian Exposition wrote to a Chicago newspaper. "The simpler the expression of art the harder it is to obtain," the architect Daniel Burnham went on. He pointed out that Americans had once imagined they could start a new school of architecture without reference to the past. It would be unavailing, he thought, to say hereafter that classic forms were undesirable. Americans had seen the vision and words could not efface it. Designers would be obliged to abandon their "incoherent originalities" and study the ancient masters of building.

The "curse of originality," which Richardson had laid on the land and his admirer Sullivan still believed in, was effectively stifled for two generations by the Chicago Fair of 1893—but not without a struggle. Artists had not learned the value of teamwork until this extraordinary event in the history of American culture had taken place. Nor had they any broad conception of city planning. But the Fair taught cooperation and the value of an overall plan. When George B. Post, one of the architects of the Fair, proposed a dome 450 feet high for his Manufactures and Liberal Arts Building, there was a murmur from his colleagues sufficient to cause him to modify the design; and when they saw Charles McKim's portico projecting over the terrace, mere looks made him withdraw it to the face of his building. Not that the buildings came out all alike; they were as different as could be, even to the Viollet-le-Duc-trained eye of Henry Van Brunt. But the picturesque was left to the lakes of Jackson Park, which Olmsted had recommended as the site for the Fair. By this time the Olmsted office had taken in the talented Henry Sargent Codman, who knew how to lay out a piece of formal work and get the proportions right; he was allowed to move Burnham's proposed fountain from the north-south axis, placing it farther back. George Peabody, also of Boston, proposed a canal to be carried down between the buildings, which became a favorite walk when illuminated at night. Adler and Sullivan were given the Transportation Building outside the Court of Honor; whereas the latter, by agreement, was sprayed white, Sullivan made his entrance a golden arch, picked out in strong colors of red and orange. Much more popular was Hunt's Administration Building, which, fittingly enough, was the focus of the whole show and managed to be monumental without being by any means the largest structure; it was the placing which helped to achieve this effect. Designers were learning the importance of a comprehensive plan. Hunt died two years later, his mission in American architecture and planning accomplished. (*See Reading No. 19.*)

The Court of Honor taught most of the classical lesson. No previous description prepared one for the first sight of it. The English author of Baedeker's Guide to the United States, James F. Muirhead, said, "We had expected that America would produce the largest, most costly and most gorgeous of international exhibitions"; but he found an air both of spontaneity and inevitableness, which suggested nature itself rather than art. It was incredible to him that America could produce anything so inexpressibly poetic, chaste, and restrained. And this in "Porkopolis," a city supposed to be given over entirely to the worship of Mammon! French admirers expressed pleasure that Americans had gotten over their love for the "merely colossal" and realized that art was important. They noted that sculptors and painters had been given as prominent a role as architects in telling the story of the Fair.

In fact, although some of the designers had been trained in France, the architecture was not the same as that being built in any European country. This is an important point, since most criticisms of the Fair's influence, including that of Louis Sullivan, are based on the erroneous idea that American architects, especially those from the East, were merely copying what they had seen abroad. The architecture and city planning of the Fair actually influenced European cities, which were in some cases about to build new civic centers and open up new squares. As the distinguished critic Talbot Hamlin has pointed out, it was a classicism which sought esthetic, not archaeological, harmony. It leaned much more to the Roman than to the French Renaissance, yet it used Renaissance forms freely. It was a flexible style, which could make a unity of a building by combining a boldness of plan with refinement of detail. It made possible the handling of entirely new building types, frequently of great scale, that a growing democracy required. These were the new state capitols, the railroad stations, and the public libraries, which are part of America's contributions to world architecture. McKim, Mead, and White's Boston Public Library, rising across Copley Square from Richardson's Trinity Church, marks the change. This classical building was completed two years after the Fair had made its impact on American life and art. (*See Reading No. 20.*)

It remained for Henry Adams, perhaps the foremost representative of the intellectual life of the country, to sum up. The Fair made us ashamed of our ignorance, he said, and the babbling futility of the society which produced such ignorance. Here was a breach in continuity . . . a rupture in historical sequence. "Chicago was the first expression of American thought as a unity," he concluded. "One must start there."

Precedents and Antecedents. Although the public was convinced that the White City was the model it wanted to follow, there was not much evidence of its type of plan to be seen, and much less of the cooperative spirit it reflected. The modern city had come into being with little thought being given to its appearance, and none to the coordination of its various parts. The gridiron was too easy to follow; and the surveyors favored it as much as the promoters of railroads, who were still bringing "civilization" to the West and risking their private capital to create towns. The donation of lots for a mill or a store would provide a shipping and receiving center, bringing more business to the line. The railroad directors wanted permanent settlements, and often would donate land for a church. Some lines, like the Burlington, which was given over two-and-one-half million acres by the government in Iowa and Nebraska, developed their own real estate corporations to buy up land where stations were plotted.

Apart from the occasional railroad plazas, which often took the place of town squares (a pretty example can still be seen at Pine City, Minnesota), the attractions of railroad-created towns were few. Even their names were chosen in a businesslike way: "I shall have two or three more towns to name very soon," wrote the promoter of a town west of Ottumwa, Iowa, during the second railroad age. "They should be short and easily pronounced. Frederic I think is a very good name. It is now literally a cornfield, so I cannot have it surveyed, but yesterday a man came to arrange to put a hotel there. This is a great country for hotels." [1]

Frederic cannot be found on a modern map of Iowa, but its type existed in the hundreds by 1890. The curving railroads only added complications to the U.S. Land Survey grid. In Modesto, California the Southern Pacific laid out the town plan oriented to the line, whereas the surrounding towns are oriented to the north-south survey. Since California politics were dominated by the railroads until 1910, when Governor Hiram Johnson's administration made their control of votes impossible, their owners could plant towns where they willed. They could bargain with existing towns, knowing that their terms would have to be met if the town did not want to be bypassed. Their directors cared no more about the wishes and feelings of the state, thought Bryce, writing in 1888, "than an English bondholder cares about the feelings of Chile." And the California author and satirist Ambrose Bierce liked to identify Leland Stanford, first president of the Central Pacific Railroad and later U.S. Senator from California, as £eland $tanford. (*See Readings Nos. 21 and 22.*)

Other corporation-built towns which mark the period were scarcely reflective of an altruistic spirit, either. Developed by necessity for mining or industrial purposes, their owners gave much less attention to the architecture than the Boston Associates had to Lowell, Massachusetts, in the 1820's, when they built handsome brick rows to house the farm girls who came to the mills. When George M. Pullman came to build his "Model Town" in 1884 in what is now Chicago's far South Side, he had no such intentions for the housing of his Palace Car factory operatives. The three-story tenements, or "block-houses" as they were called, had three to five hundred people under one roof, because of the need to take in lodgers to meet the high rents, with sometimes only one faucet to every five families. Although the town was designed by the architect Solon S. Beman of the Chicago School, the local architects of that day paid more attention to the designing of office buildings and hotels than to

[1] Richard C. Overton, *Burlington West* (Cambridge, Mass., 1941), p. 184.

housing projects. Their historian, Carl Condit, gives the Chicago
School credit for modernizing the hotel: such features as continuous circulation of steam heat and hot water, built-in service
furniture, and the safe-deposit vault at the reception desk were
among their innovations.

In spite of Pullman's failure as a city planner (after the notorious Pullman strike of 1894 the Supreme Court of Illinois ruled
that the company could not hold real estate beyond that necessary
for the business of manufacturing), it was still the age of the
millionaire rather than the city corporation. In the panic of 1893,
it was Marshall Field who honored small depositors' bank ac-
counts at his store in Chicago, and other millionaires who, in
making their charitable contributions, enabled Jane Addams' Hull
House, the Symphony Orchestra, the Art Institute, and the University of Chicago to weather the storm.[2]

It was the last-named institution that the millionaires loved
to help. New campuses were springing up all over the country,
and many were founded by the financiers themselves. When
Leland Stanford left over twenty million dollars to establish a
university in memory of his son, he and others like him provided
an opportunity for the designers to experiment with the grand
design principles of the Fair. In fact, Olmsted and his son John,
who had joined him in practice, anticipated formal planning
when they designed the Leland Stanford, Jr. campus in 1886.
This was laid out on land next to Menlo Park at Palo Alto,
and was centered on a strong axis and cross-axis, contrasting
with the elder Olmsted's picturesque plan for the University of
California at Berkeley twenty years before. Olmsted thus repudi-
ated his former contention that "symmetrical arrangement" is a
cause of "great inconvenience and perplexity."

More direct influence of the Fair can be seen in Henry Ives
Cobb's plan for American University in Washington, D.C., where
the buildings enclose space rather than just sit in space. Others
turned for inspiration to Union College, Schenectady and the
University of Virginia, where the French architect Joseph Jacques
Ramée and Thomas Jefferson respectively had laid out campuses
in the grand manner at the beginning of the nineteenth century.
When Columbia University moved uptown in 1897, it was to
Jefferson's "academical village" that the architects McKim, Mead,

[2] Wayne Andrews, *Battle for Chicago* (New York, 1946), p. 153.

and White turned for inspiration, giving their library building
the central position. Johns Hopkins, another example of a private donor's founding an institution of higher learning in his own
city, Baltimore, also developed a formal plan, the type which
was to be used throughout the next generation, as American
colleges turned themselves into universities under the influence
of new educational theories.

European Influences. Since education was being influenced
by Germanic and other theorists, it might be supposed that new
city-planning ideas from abroad would condition American ap-
proaches to shaping the environment; but apart from French
methods of composition brought over by the architects who had
studied at the Beaux-Arts, Americans had very little interest
in contemporary European precedent. In Germany, which was
to play a role in the development of American city planning
somewhat later, planning engineers dominated the scene. One
of these, Rheinhard Baumeister, first laid down the law that
city planning was a function of vehicular traffic, a one-sided
view which has since been the curse of any city subscribing to
it. Otherwise he suggested that streets be gently curved to avoid
monotony, a prescription to which the Olmsted firm returned
again and again. Another German planner, Joseph Stübben,
worked for more than thirty cities in that country and took part
in many international conferences, among them the Chicago
World's Fair, where his paper on artistic planning and the
placing of monuments seems to have made little stir among the
engineers present. According to the art historian George Collins,
Stübben was scornful of American planning, except for the Parks
Movement, until this country began to show an interest in
German zoning ordinances later in the period.

The Austrian Camillo Sitte also had to wait for his influence
to penetrate the United States. In fact he could not wait, dying
in 1903. A fervent admirer of Richard Wagner, he felt that art
must have a national basis to be great, and nursed a secret
project to build a huge tower devoted to the display of German
creativity, much as Patrick Geddes planned his Outlook Tower
in Edinburgh to record city planning through the ages. He
despised French culture; and his book, published in German
in 1889, has been taken as an anti-Haussmann polemic. Admirers, who have been many, have nevertheless argued as to

whether Sitte was promoting Baroque city planning or a return to the medieval "informality" in squares and arrangements of buildings. Addressed mainly to a Viennese audience, the book attacked the official plans for the Vienna Ring, suggesting a series of interrelated squares, instead of the boulevards intersecting at awkward angles that were actually built.

Neither did the English Garden City movement affect American planning until well into the first decade of the twentieth century. George M. Pullman's model had been the paternalistic housing projects of the Krupp family at Essen; the town of Pullman, Illinois, preceded Bourneville and Port Sunlight in England, built respectively by the Cadburys and Levers a few years later. Rather, it was Edward Bellamy, with his *Looking Backward,* and other American socialists who influenced Ebenezer Howard, the father of the Garden City movement in England, to burst into print in 1898 with *Tomorrow: A Peaceful Path to Real Reform. (See Readings Nos. 23 and 24.)* Architecturally, also, the transatlantic influence ran from west to east. Publication of American work in English magazines caused excitement in the School of Architecture at Liverpool. Its historian recorded that American work seemed to have "all the breadth of the French with the refinement of the Italian, and yet was wonderfully Anglo-Saxon." The plan of the first Garden City at Letchworth, near London, "has something of the City Beautiful axiality," according to Walter Creese, historian of the Garden City. By the turn of the century the City Beautiful movement was in full swing in the United States.

By 1909, the most important outside influence came from English Garden City architects. Raymond Unwin's book *Town Planning in Practice,* published in that year, lays an emphasis on group planning for housing. (Unwin and Barry Parker had designed Letchworth Garden City in 1904.) But in his preface to the second edition in 1911, Unwin stresses the importance of American planning, mentioning "the wonderful drawings for Washington and Chicago, showing a grasp and breadth of treatment quite American in its scale."

The Revival of Planning in Washington.   As a triumph for the American architectural profession, the White City could not have been surpassed. That stunning composition, which had pleased the public even more than the small band of critics, had been achieved entirely by native artists. American architects were henceforth looked at with more esteem. It was logical that they should be called in for important public work. With Hunt's death a new leader appeared in Charles Follen McKim, a superb designer, whose younger partner Stanford White, a much gayer ornament of the New York social world, often eclipsed him in popularity. But McKim's great Boston Public Library, on the decoration of which he employed leading painters like John Singer Sargent and Puvis de Chavannes, and the University Club on Fifth Avenue in New York, one of the finest buildings ever to grace that city, still stand as testimony to his genius. The firm's biographer, Sir Charles Reilly, however, cautions against ascribing the firm's work exclusively to any one master. He found them a group of self-denying artists, who expressed "the finest aspirations of a great people at a great epoch."

It was logical then for Daniel Burnham and Frederick Law Olmsted (a son of the same name as the father) to call in McKim when they were appointed to the Senate Park Commission in 1901. This was to prepare plans for the park system of the District of Columbia. Assisted by the sculptor St. Gaudens, the team studied the layout of Williamsburg as well as famous malls in Europe, producing plans for the Washington Mall— the main outlines of which we see today, Rock Creek Park, and other open spaces. (*See Readings Nos. 25 and 26.*)

Naturally enough, attention focussed on the Mall. This was L'Enfant's "Grand Avenue" of 1791, a mile long and 400 feet wide, now to be over double the width and lined with four rows of trees on either side. The new plan was a plan for a park. Since L'Enfant left no drawings for the architecture, and his description is vague (the Grand Avenue was to be "bordered with gardens, ending in a slope from the houses on each side"), the new planners can be pardoned for changing the scale. This time the frame was not to be houses, but great public buildings. The widened mall could afford these. Beyond the Washington Monument, the Mall was to end in the Lincoln Memorial, with a long pool between the two.

Designed in New York, in special offices above those of McKim, Mead, and White, the plan was an instant success. Over four times longer than the Court of Honor at Chicago, and im-

mensely wide, the scheme nevertheless brought back the essence
of the L'Enfant Grand Avenue, which had been violated by
pre-Civil War romantic gardening, the placing forward of the
architect Renwick's Smithsonian Institution, and the running
of a railroad track down the empty open space. Burnham persuaded Alexander Cassatt, president of the Pennsylvania Railroad, to remove the tracks from the Mall, the latter responding
by having Burnham design Union Station, the first grand
terminus of the new century. And the axis of the Mall was
shifted slightly to center on the casually-placed Washington
Monument, the site of which was cleared of trees so that for the
first time it could rise majestic and unobscured.

The weakest part of the new plan was the treatment of Lafayette Square as a rebuilt setting for the White House, which
was not recognized for the rather modest mansion that it is.
Although we do not seem to be treating its architecture much
better today, Lafayette Square should have remained what it
then was—surrounded by old houses, a Latrobe church, and
other low-scaled buildings. Except for this fortunately unrealized
proposal, the heart of Washington was restored to its original
plan; and a new pride arose in the American past. Would this
new pride sufficiently enflame the American? wondered Henry
James. Although the "formal majesty" of the plan seemed as-
sured, he warned that the carrying out of any plan in this
country always had to survive new and incalculable risks. This
time, he thought, the grand gesture would be made; and he
lived to see in the next decade such an effort made to create a
worthy environment as had never been encountered before on
any comparable scale.

The Age of Reform. The American situation was quite
special, mused the Scottish planner Patrick Geddes in 1904.
Looking out from his tower in Edinburgh, he pitied the American citizen "struggling with abuses on one hand, and carrying
out his ideals with vast wealth upon the other." It was a land of
contrasts, lacking a settled civic system and badly in need of
a social conscience. "Make an intelligent visit to the market
place of Brussels, the Hotel de Ville of Ghent and the Belfry
of Bruges," he advised Americans; there lessons could be learned
from the medieval civic revival. His disciple Lewis Mumford
has since sounded an even louder note on the excellences of

the medieval world in architecture and as a way of life; and in an influential book, *The Culture of Cities,* he praises medieval town planning over what are to him the excesses of ancient Rome and of the Renaissance.

It was perhaps inevitable that reformers like William Morris in England and Thorstein Veblen in America should admire the medieval "instinct of workmanship" that they thought essential to the citizen's self-fulfilment, and should despise, in turn, the mechanization of life and thought which the advanced capitalist society seemed to be producing. The "bigness" of the machine-dominated world frightened those, who, like Jane Addams, were trying to improve the lot of the factory worker; and to many of them the small round of medieval life as they imagined it to have been had great appeal. When the Garden Cities came to be built in England, groups of maypole dancers were organized; and much was made of social activities centered on the village green.

If the aloof Veblen, critic and analyst of the leisure class, taught some people to dislike ornament and other manifestations of "conspicuous waste," there were men and women in the tidal wave of reform who turned to the sore spots, practicing what they preached by working and living in the slums and overcrowded tenements of the big cities. There was the "social church"; and although in many instances its chief function seemed to be conversion of immigrants to a new faith, many a clergyman and social worker learned what needed to be done by tramping the streets, as Jacob Riis and Theodore Roosevelt did on New York's teeming East Side. The Salvation Army helped to spread tolerance as well as charity, introducing its "slum brigades" in the 1890's when the tenement situation was at its worst. Ida M. Tarbell and Upton Sinclair took their muck-rakes into industry, an Augean stable of injustices at the time. Possibly the intellectual who learned most about the city was Lincoln Steffens; giving up a gilded background, he too learned the hard way, as a reporter. Eventually he came to understand that the conditions he found in a particular city were not pecul-iar to itself, but were often generic. He came to look at the city, not as an artifact as Emerson and others had done, but as a dynamic growth, realizing that there was a common problem of civilized living in human communities, and that cities could only forge ahead with the help of the people. For this reason, he thought, leaders should be men whom the people trust; men like Ben Lindsay, the Democratic judge in Denver, "who applied Christianity in the courtroom" and was kept in office by the votes of the poor; or Everett Colby, the rich young Wall Street broker, who beat the New Jersey bosses in a final showdown. Steffens explained the social system in the cities to his readers, noting that the good man in business often turned out to be the bad man in politics. And although he admired reform mayors like Tom Johnson and "Golden Rule" Jones, he realized that reform politics was still politics. "Only worse," he was forced to add. Reformers were not so smooth as the professional politicians, and it seemed to him they were not so honest. He valued intelligence highly and warned that the sincerity of dedicated people would never be enough to erase the shame of the cities.

If political reform was constantly running into obstacles in the form of influential persons—bosses, the new union leaders, local magnates—and powerful groups such as party organizations, "vested interests," lobbies, unions, and manufacturers associations, the plodding pace of housing reform could better be put down to ignorance and inertia. The lesson Steffens learned—that the slum was more than a physical setting—was not understood in the early days of the housing movement. The Tenement House Law of 1901, reducing the density and requiring a bathroom in every *apartment,* did not prevent more than one family from crowding into the apartment. The slum was a way of life, not merely streets and buildings; it was even a state of mind, as Robert E. Park was fond of reminding his sociology students. Accepting the relationship between housing and social control as a matter of faith, reformers of that day could only think of eradicating windowless rooms with the aid of housing inspectors; and while model tenements were built after the "New Law" was passed, they were few in number and the "housing question" remained unsolved. Those mayors who, like "Golden Rule" Jones in Toledo, Ohio, introduced free kindergartens into the public schools, built playgrounds, and granted the eight-hour day for city employees, probably were accomplishing more to solve "the common problems of civilized living in human communities" than Governor Odell and his Tenement

House Law of 1901. Lawrence Veiller, the housing reformer
who was responsible for it, always regarded the bill as a compro-
mise. Although it effected some reforms, Veiller hoped that
the city might be purified by fire, and that whole sections
might thus be destroyed. The Tenement House Department
of the City of New York removed some of the filth and repaired
the dilapidation; but as late as 1929, according to George Ford's
classic *Slums and Housing,* there had been comparatively little
advancement in the design of tenements on Manhattan since
the architect Ernest Flagg had first advocated larger unit
construction in 1894. Flagg, who also figures importantly in the
development of the tower-form skyscraper, is considered to be
the father of the modern tenement. (*See Readings Nos. 27
and 28.*)

The Urban World of J. P. Morgan. The citizen whom
Patrick Geddes described as "carrying out his ideals with vast
wealth," was able to do so with the rise of the corporation and
of what came to be called "international banking." J. P. Morgan's
leadership of the New York money market until 1910, symbolized by the rise of private banking houses and their control of
railroad, utility, and industrial investment, depended on reliable
foreign connections, the domestic market being uncertain.
Morgan had Drexel, Morgan in Philadelphia and New York, his
father's banking house in London, and Morgan, Harjes in Paris
all behind him. Whenever Morgan lent his name to a syndicate,
one could be sure that the business would be well-managed.
Big business thus went hand and hand with big finance. In the
prosperous years from 1897 to 1904, the rate of formation of
big companies accelerated. Helped by Morgan, Lee, Higginson,
and other private banks, Morgan assembled the necessary capital
for the creation of the giant U.S. Steel Corporation in 1901.
Having saved the credit of the government itself in the Panic
of 1893, Morgan's interests grew so wide that a year before he
died his affiliated banks had directorships in 112 corporations
with resources of over twenty-two billion dollars.

New companies meant new office buildings. The reorganization of corporate structure allowed business to regionalize itself;
and many a city acquired offices of a company headquartered
in New York, St. Louis, or San Francisco. New bank buildings
arose, classical decoration being favored by their presidents.

New York wrested from Chicago the title of having the tallest building, when early in 1899 George B. Post's St. Paul Building was completed, a classical skyscraper with clustered pilasters on every floor, a columned entrance, and rich ornament on the topmost stories. His New York Stock Exchange, built between 1901 and 1904 and a much finer structure, had a sculptured pediment and Corinthian columns behind which rose the first glass curtain wall in New York, providing light for the great floor of the Exchange. There was also a new wave of hotel building, New York's St. Regis by the architects Trowbridge and Livingston being the most handsomely decorated. Its ornamental bronze doors still welcome the visitor on arrival.

Then there were the libraries, with New York's consolidation of the old Astor Library, the Lenox Library, and the Tilden Foundation into one world-famous Public Library at Fifth Avenue and Forty-second Street. In 1898 the architects Carrere and Hastings won the competition for this building and took care that New Yorkers would have beautifully-detailed walls and ceilings on which to rest their eyes. Thomas Hastings designed the bronze flagpole bases for the terrace outside; they are among the best examples of the decorative arts in the country. Among his collected writings can be found evidence of the architect's faith in the power of beauty to influence the lives of urban dwellers. "Beauty creates an atmosphere in its environment which breeds the proper kind of contentment," he wrote, "that kind of contentment which stimulates ambition." If we would be modern, he advised young architects, we must realize that beauty of design in line and construction builds well and with greater economy and endurance than construction which is mere engineering. "Will disorder and confusion in our modern architecture express the intelligence of this twentieth century?" he wondered, as if aware of the rebellious small voice of Secessionism beginning to be heard in Munich and Vienna.

But under the presidencies of Theodore Roosevelt and William Howard Taft the face of the land was to be made beautiful; and what was created in the San Francisco Civic Center, begun in 1912, could stand on its own beside the Vienna Ring or the Carlsplatz in Munich. Designers had learned that the ensemble of carefully calculated relationships in scale and proportion was what made the city "read." When Carrere and Hastings came to make a plan for the city of Hartford, they pointed to the case of Washington, where, with all its faults, a comprehensive plan was being followed, with attempts to have the buildings in size and scale "pleasingly related to each other." This did not prevent the architect-planners from consideration of vehicular-traffic problems and even of the possibilities of air travel.

This was the age in which the big city held its greatest attractions, and New York topped the list. It was elegant and fashionable. More houses of the rich appeared on Fifth Avenue and the streets nearby. One can tell they were built for entertaining by examining the plans. The first and second floors of these town houses contained libraries, dining rooms, drawing rooms, and ballrooms, which, together with the staircase halls, were as generous as the architect could make them. The third and fourth floors were for the family, and then there was the servants' attic, a little more generous than in the past; for in the age of Edith Wharton and Henry James, no one was really uncomfortable. Such a house was that built for Otto Kahn on 91st Street by Warren and Wetmore, who were soon to obtain the commission for the new Grand Central Station. The development of Park Avenue was still in the future.

In spite of the fact that, because of the rise of the corporation, the early financiers were being replaced by boards of directors, they still kept their role of client when it came to dealing with architects. "Jupiter" Morgan built his great urban library in 1905-1906, retaining McKim, Mead, and White for this design and also for the American Academy in Rome, which he built and supported. There went the talented young American designers to study the classical and Renaissance past. Many critics think nothing actually surpassed the Villard Mansion on Madison Avenue, a product of the McKim, Mead, and White office in the manner of an early sixteenth-century Italian palazzo. This fortunately remains, the group of four houses around a court having been converted into business offices and the headquarters of the Roman Catholic archdiocese in New York. Only the material remains to place the building as early as it is; in 1885 brownstone—"that hideous, chocolate colored building material," as Edith Wharton called it—was still in use.

Only a Morgan could have built his exquisite library, with its stones perfectly fitted in the masonry walls—a lost art today

—and filled it with the rare and costly items that remain in it for our pleasure. "Evidently," marveled Count Boni de Castellane, a latter-day French visitor to New York, "Americans prefer giants to men of mere human proportions." Their genius was still chaotic, he thought, and their strength immeasurable. Not having ancestors, they did not think much about creating an inheritance. This was not strictly true, since Morgan was to leave a financial dynasty and, more important, a rule of taste that stands as a measure of our artistic failures today. Count de Castellane noted that Americans built railroad stations like palaces, not realizing that they were to set a standard for public meeting-places all over the world, not only in their architecture but in their engineering advances. Thomas Wolfe, writing much later, found something American as well as something lasting about these giant termini, in which the sound of a locomotive was seldom heard, the train shed being separated from the waiting room. Instead, young Tom found "the calm voice of time" echoing softly there along the walls and ceilings of a "mighty room." No Macaenas had ever built a palace to equal Grand Central Station (1903-1913), a public gathering-place of unheard-of scale and magnificence.

Now that the railroad age is over and termini will never be built again in quite this way, Americans are beginning to include them in a sense of the past of which they can be proud. Not only the architecture will be remembered. It was an age of tremendous advance in science, now belatedly achieving its proper place in the history of medicine, for instance. To its literature the pundits return again and again. Against the advances made in welfare, industrial growth, farming, and architecture, criticisms of its preoccupation with material wealth grow dimmer with the years. If Veblen railed against the public buildings, saying that they represented only a taste for costliness masquerading under the name of beauty, he was answered by Santayana, who pointed out that cost indeed had something to do with size in architecture, and that extravagance was a recognized prerogative of all the arts. When, a few years later, Theodore Dreiser wrote his trilogy of novels which includes *The Titan,* it was a traction ring operator Charles T. Yerkes, plunderer of the Chicago street railways and with a prison record, who was the "hero." The contrast with a man like

Morgan, who made it a practice never to charge more than 6 percent interest on a loan, is startling. The United States had produced a new crop of educated businessmen; and while the entrepreneur continued to flourish, there were those who knew their duty to society and performed it well. Morgan died in Rome in 1913, just as the changes to be wrought by mass production were beginning to be felt in urban life. With him died the age of elegance and the period in which the city wore a classic smile.

Turn-of-the-Century Cities. It was still the classic city in another sense of the term. City-suburb-country were well defined entities; and if the first two were growing, they did not occupy space far from the railroad network. Industrial workers had to live not far from the works themselves, which accounted not only for the building of manufacturing plants in cities, but in satellite communities like Andrew Carnegie's Homestead, eight miles outside Pittsburgh on the Monongahela River. The workers' village huddled round the great industrial plant was a familiar sight before the advent of personalized transportation. It was the grimmest sight to be seen on the face of the American landscape, but no grimmer than the hidden slums of the great cities which only a few cared to investigate.

Nevertheless, some cities had grown so big as to demand political reorganization. Although Los Angeles had jumped from 50,000 people in 1890 to 102,000 in 1900, and was to triple that population by 1910, it was not yet in the class which made consolidation tempting. New York, however, with 1,500,000 people in 1890, was being made to realize that it was part of an area called "Greater" New York with a total population of nearly three times that number, including Brooklyn, the country's fourth largest city. In 1898 Greater New York began its consolidated life, partly the result of promotion during the previous thirty years by Andrew Haswell Green, a former member of the New York Park Board. There had been a previous annexation of three western townships in the Bronx; and the opening of the Brooklyn Bridge in 1883 provided a further impetus to Green and his followers, who eventually overcame sentiments for an independent Brooklyn and won their victory with the help of Thomas C. Platt, the leader of the Republican state party organization. The borough system that resulted made New York's government very different from that of, say, the ward politics of Philadelphia and Chicago. Inherently conservative, according to the political scientists Wallace Sayre and Herbert Kaufman, New York's system provides opportunities for leadership by a variety of participants and is committed to bargaining and accommodation—a far cry from the days of Boss Tweed and his Ring.

It was natural that the focus on governmental reform should reveal problems which the city retained in its fabric. This, and the McMillan Commission's Plan for Washington, together with the much older parks movement, served to point up the urgency of comprehensive planning that Richard Morris Hunt had foreseen at the Philadelphia Centennial. Traffic, transit, and transportation had become a public concern. Problems of circulation arose wherever cities expanded, helping to crowd the older centers with shoppers and office workers from the outskirts. If the bloody Homestead Strike of 1892 had checked the rise of unionism in steel for several decades, there were city-based unions like the International Ladies Garment Workers, founded in 1900 with 2,000 members, which began to take an interest in employees' housing. Members of the Progressive municipal reform movement like Benjamin C. Marsh, a Henry George single-taxer interested in land problems, pointed out the need for the relief of congestion. The population of Manhattan rose from 1,850,000 in 1900 to 2,321,000 by 1910, and the density of people per acre to 166.1. Marsh organized New York's first exhibition on congestion in 1908, and, partly because of the resulting publicity, the first national conference on city planning in Washington a year later. Much stress was laid on economics there, Marsh emphasizing the importance of a technical survey of industrial conditions, housing needs, and the ownership and control of land, as might be expected from his background. His city-planning ideas, reflected in the New York Congestion Commission's report of 1911, included restriction on the height and lot coverage of buildings, a reduction of taxation on buildings to prevent speculative holding of land, and extension of public transportation to encourage migration to the suburbs. The philanthropist Robert Treat Paine had advocated the last-named device for Boston workers. "Go and live at the end of the trolley line," he advised, "where the air is healthier." Marsh went further, suggesting that immigrants should be encouraged to adopt agriculture as a way of life, heralding subsequent "back-to-the-land" movements which reached their climax in the depression of the 1930's.

Thus the concept of decentralization of the city was introduced at the very start of the city-planning movement in the United States. We shall see what the consequences were for the city itself in Chapter 7.

The City Beautiful Movement in Practice. Meanwhile, the architects were refining their plans, joined in a few cases by landscape architects and civil engineers. Daniel Burnham, who admonished Chicago speculators in his own way by pointing out that "the relationship of all the buildings is more important than anything else," was called in to make a plan for San Francisco. This city with expansion had become a series of refracted grids and was clearly in need of an orderly street system, if nothing more.[3] Burnham, now with a collaborator Edward H. Bennett, undertook his municipal planning work without a fee, in this case at the invitation of the Association for the Improvement and Adornment of San Francisco and John D. Phelan, former mayor and United States Senator from California. A report was published in 1905, and then came the earthquake. Although Burnham was hurriedly called back from a European vacation, such was the impetus to rebuild quickly that not a vestige of his plan was carried out, the famous Civic Center being built later on another site. But the planning work done for San Francisco was a rehearsal, and a useful one, for the much more important Chicago plan which was to follow. It should be pointed out here that Burnham did plan civic centers, notably that complex known as The Mall in Cleveland, where he was less successful in persuading a lake-front railroad to move its tracks than he had been with the trains on the Mall in Washington. A smaller civic center by Burnham can be found at Duluth, Minnesota. There, in the tangy, northern atmosphere of this end-of-the-line shipping center, with the ore boats of United States Steel sweeping in from Lake Superior, the Chicago planner's classical buildings add

---

[3] After O'Farrell's survey in 1847, speculators pushed the grid all over the city. One result is that the grids north and south of the diagonal Market Street do not line up with each other, nor are the blocks the same size.

a note of serenity in a strung-out, sprawling port city which otherwise shows little architectural merit.

If Burnham and his colleagues were the giants of the City Beautiful movement, there were others to account for the proliferation of new plans for old cities which occurred after Washington and San Francisco. Los Angeles waited until 1909 and chose as its planner Charles Mulford Robinson, who became a Professor of Civic Design at the University of Illinois, and whose book, *The Improvement of Towns and Cities* (1907) had a certain influence. Robinson became one of the chief publicists of the movement, as his reports, *The Improvement of Honolulu* (1906), *The Beautifying of San Jose* (1909), bear witness. Unlike Burnham, who prepared the first comprehensive modern plan for an American city (Chicago) in the same year, Robinson usually made suggestions for parts of cities, concentrating on the park system, connected by parkways; smaller, strategically located playgrounds for children; rather modest and architecturally undistinguished civic centers; and carefully designed entrances to the city. He and others were concerned about the traffic-carrying capacities of streets (this was to develop into a positive mania for street-widening among engineer-planners), and in his plan for Los Angeles he proposed separate lanes for slow- and fast-moving traffic on a particularly heavily-used street. In Oakland he found that waterfront land was too expensive "to make practical the relinquishment of any part of it for esthetic purposes," regretting that he could not recommend a formal entrance to the city by water. His ideas for beautification included tourism and local color; in San Jose he included a small park in the Japanese manner and hoped that the nearby Oriental population would "unconsciously heighten its effectiveness" by making use of it!

Although Robinson apparently had not seen Sitte on his trip to Europe in 1899 for Harper's Magazine, many of his ideas would have met with the approval of the only important theorist of that day. In Los Angeles, a skyscraper had already been built in front of the post office, precluding as some thought any regular plan for the civic center. Robinson prepared an irregular plan, recalling that "nearly all of the best 'places' of Europe have had the charm of picturesqueness, and of curious angles, as this would have." If he had read Sitte's book, it would have been in German or French, but many of the Austrian planner's ideas had been publicized in America by Stübben.

The picturesque syndrome was not yet accepted in planning circles, and was continuing largely in the design of parks. These occupied most of the space in the growing number of planning reports, many of which were prepared by landscape architects like George E. Kessler in his city plan for Dallas or John Nolen at Roanoke, Virginia. Civic improvement groups planted street trees in the growing residential sections of cities north and south, very often these new developments being the pride of the community. Newly created park commissions often took over the responsibility for maintaining the leafy appearance of these residential avenues. Before the mass-production of automobiles these trees were relatively safe and healthy, but in recent years they have been decimated for reasons of municipal inertia, snow removal, street-widening, overhead wiring, or disease, and combinations of these factors. Gone are the elegant pepper trees from the streets of Hollywood and the elms that once graced New Haven's downtown business district, another amenity lost before the demands of unchecked machine fetishism.

Architects and planners not only had opportunities to plan civic centers, but state government centers as well. The states were outgrowing their earlier office facilities, and with the classical renaissance sweeping the country were ready to build imposing new houses for their legislators and staffs. McKim, Mead, and White designed the capitol at Providence, and Joseph M. Huston the lavishly decorated one at Harrisburg, Pennsylvania, with its high green dome and paintings by Edwin Austin Abbey. A particularly well-proportioned capitol was designed by Cass Gilbert for St. Paul, Minnesota; only in our own postwar period has the approach to it been widened, and unsympathetic neighbors have been added to the state-capitol complex there. Perhaps of all the state buildings of this period the George B. Post and Sons' Wisconsin state capitol is the most splendid, with its commanding site above the lake, rich marbles, and spacious interiors signifying that here too the classical is not to be gainsaid as the appropriate setting for the government of a great territory. As one travels the country today, the extraordinary quality of the City Beautiful architecture, not only in these government buildings, but in civic structures like clubs and banks, stands out to be admired among the blank faces of the newer commercial buildings, bereft as the latter are of ornament or any human touch in the form of sculpture or decoration. How dull would downtown Philadelphia be without the temple-like form of the Girard Trust Company and the Franklin National Bank, both by McKim, Mead, and White; how tawdry New York's 42nd Street district without the redeeming features of the Public Library and the classic formal park behind it; how unimposing Fifth Avenue as a processional way without Tiffany's, the Metropolitan Club, and the Hotel Plaza!

The First Regional Plan.   The generation of patrons which died with Morgan and the coming of World War I could never again be matched, and their designers were leaving with them. The last letter Charles Follen McKim wrote to his friend Daniel Burnham congratulated the Chicago architect on what was to be his last great work. "My dear Daniel," he wrote in 1909, ". . . the whole result of your labors (on the Chicago Improvement Plan) stands as one of your monuments—far greater than all of them put together, in fact."[4] McKim was prophetic. Burnham had been working since the late 1890's on the Chicago plan, which had begun as an idea for improving the lakefront with a boulevard, a long narrow park, and a protected lagoon for boating. It was shown to Chicago leaders at a private dinner in 1896, and many became enthusiastic, George Pullman exclaiming that he would be ready to donate his riparian rights in order to help the project. Even the cautious Marshall Field agreed that the scheme had possibilities; and if Burnham had not been so busy with other commissions, active steps would have been taken to effect it then and there. It was not until 1907 that his ideas took shape in the form later published by the Commercial Club, and although in his speeches the planner stressed the part dealing with the lakefront in order to fire local enthusiasm, the study had grown in scope to make recommendations for all the territory lying within a radius of sixty miles of Chicago, including new arteries, the cutting of new streets, regulation of traffic, the relocation of railroad terminals near a magnificent new civic center, the development of an outer park and boulevard system and even forest preserves throughout the county.

[4] As quoted in Charles Moore, *Daniel H. Burnham: Architect, Planner of Cities* (Boston and New York, 1921), Vol. II, p. 112.

CHAPTER 6

Plans and Planners, 1910-1930

Growing without Pain. Although the need for city planning had been stressed by Richard Morris Hunt a generation before, it was only after the first decade of the twentieth century that cities began to accept it as a function of local government. For although it was possible to trace "Metropolitan Improvement" back to the early years of the nineteenth century in London, this had meant functional operations like bridge-building, water supply or road construction; and nothing like a comprehensive plan such as Burnham's for Chicago had been conceived until nineteenth-century Paris provided an early model. Also, the American parks movement, which had gained world-wide attention while Olmsted was alive, in part substituted for other needs that were blithely overlooked until 1910. Housing legislation was mainly restrictive, and it was only at about that time that low-cost government loans to assist in home-building began to be discussed. Transportation problems were noticeable, and were taken care of, it was agreed, largely by street-widening. But it was not until 1913 that the first automobile assembly plant, built by Henry Ford, began the mass-production of automobiles. The New York City zoning ordinance was not adopted until 1916; and while it had far-reaching effects, such as putting Harlem into a straitjacket of commercial avenues and residential side streets, its defenders could not justly claim it as a comprehensive planning measure.

It was, however, during the period 1910 to 1930 that the seeds of the City Practical were sown. Its wretched harvest was reaped in the 1930's in the era of Robert Moses, while the present generation is left gazing at the stubble, wondering what to do next. The fact that official city-planning boards—established by legislative act, and which began to be established after 1907 (Hartford, Connecticut, was the first)—were not effective in creating a planned environment deserves some explanation.

First and foremost, American society was not ready to accept the constraints that planning might put on individual initiative.

Robert Walker points out in his book *The Planning Function in Urban Government* that despite a predominantly architectural emphasis, the Chicago plan, like the first national planning conference, held in Washington the same year in which the plan was published, "proposed a synthesis of physical and social planning too far in advance of current social and political attitudes to find immediate acceptance.[1] It was a free-wheeling age; and although President Theodore Roosevelt had shaken a big stick against the trusts, the period before the federal income-tax law (1916) and the first housing crisis (1918-1920) was the last to feel safe in the comfortable world of finance capitalism. The railroads reached their peak of trackage by 1916, and only after that year began their steady decline. The United States reluctantly entered World War I in 1917, and before its end had four-and-one-half million men in the armed forces, half of these inducted through Selective Service. Still, Americans could not believe that the age of regulation had begun. The crisis of the farmers and the greatest battles for collective bargaining still lay ahead.

Although planners themselves moved from land-use proposals having to do solely with public lands and sites toward transportation matters, zoning (after 1916), and areas of the city where private ownership dominated, they were seldom able to implement a rational land-use plan for the community. Zoning quickly caught on as a method of eliminating undesirable uses and improving land values. However, the idea that government should interfere with private interests except to aid them in achieving their own goals was still quite foreign to the business world. A notable example of this attitude was the unwillingness of the federal government to initiate a program of public power ownership and operation on the Tennessee River after World War I. The war had forced the government into the nitrate and power business, and in 1918 a dam was started at Muscle Shoals. Afterwards, an effort was made to dispose of the properties there to private interests; but when Henry Ford offered only five million dollars for an investment which had a scrap value of over eight million, such a sale would have been too embarrassing to

[1] Robert Averill Walker, *The Planning Function in Urban Government,* 2nd ed. (Chicago, 1950), p. 19.

close. The forerunner of the electric utilities company that later became Commonwealth and Southern made a similar offer. In spite of the fact that it was becoming apparent that the government was the sole agency able to finance the development, attempts were made to give away the properties all through the 1920's. Senator George W. Norris, the Nebraska Progressive, introduced his first bill for the national development of the Tennessee River in 1922, forecasting the TVA bill of eleven years later. His sixth bill passed both Houses, but in 1931 it was vetoed by President Hoover. But his successor was interested in regional planning and knew the problems of the area from his visits to Warm Springs, Georgia. Partly because Governor Roosevelt needed Norris's support in this presidential campaign and also because he had opposed the power interests as governor of New York State, a seventh bill, creating the famous Tennessee Valley Authority, was introduced during the Hundred Days.

Without the possibility of remaking the cities, there was nevertheless work for the planners to do in laying out the new "Garden Suburbs." This term was an echo of the Garden City ideal. Letchworth, the first Garden City, had been laid out in 1904, along the lines that Ebenezer Howard had suggested in his book, *Tomorrow: A Peaceful Path to Real Reform*, published in 1898. Called by the American housing expert, Catherine Bauer, many years later, "a thorough-going experiment in consumer cooperation," Letchworth had vested all land in the hands of a board of trustees; and profits from the ground rents were ploughed back into community in the form of civic buildings, parks, and extra amenities. However, the wealthy suburbs that grew up before the automobile age of the late twenties and early thirties in this country were gardened only physically and were in no sense the satellite cities that the English precedent had set. New suburb developments like Babson Park, Wellesley, Massachusetts, or the Country Club District of Kansas City, Missouri, might evince some interesting features in their plan, like the shopping center in the latter example; but the residents were seldom stockholders in the real estate corporations that created them. (*See Readings Nos. 29 and 30.*)

Planners were also hired to lay out new industrial towns, which sprang up in this first era of mass-production and mass-distribution. These might or might not be company-controlled, but they were all built privately by families or corporations. Gary, Indiana (1905-1907), built on land owned by the United States Steel Corporation, is perhaps the best known, after 1921 becoming a typical modern industrial city. Some of these communities could even be called good-looking. The Draper textile family maintained high standards through the years at Hopedale, Massachusetts, employing expert advice in our own day from the Boston town planner, Arthur A. Shurcliff. The tradition of exemplary design stems from the earliest days of industrial towns in Massachusetts, Lowell being the prototype. Although the red-brick urbanity of the early part of Lowell was not matched in the towns built in the early years of this century, many of them attempted within the modes and taste of their own age to achieve a standard of appearance. Budgett Meakin, in his book, *Model Factories and Villages* (1905) praises Hopedale for its 150 acres of park, its electrical and sanitary facilities, and in the newer parts "the way the roads are curved, to avoid the wearying sameness of the interminable American streets, and are all planted with trees." The picturesque manner was catching on at last, and presently was going to replace the classic revival then in full command. That this manner gained ground first in the suburbs, under Garden City influence, is especially to be noted.

Most promoters of company towns, and even philanthropic agencies, although they might hire planners or landscape architects for their ground plan, exhibited a woeful neglect of architectural design. An exception is Forest Hills Gardens (1911) financed by the Russell Sage Foundation as a business enterprise expected to return a reasonable return on the investment, but also to show what could be accomplished by real estate in comprehensive planning. Deciding not to build "a suburb for laboring people with low wages" because of the cost of the land, which was only eight miles from Pennsylvania Station on the Long Island Railroad, the Sage Foundation Homes Co. nevertheless said it would not be greedy, "to take the last cent out of its clients." It would not permit lot owners to build unsightly houses, however, and employed the town planner, Frederick Law Olmsted, Jr. and the architect Grosvenor Atterbury to design many of the buildings. It is noteworthy that one Clarence A. Perry of the Foundation later proposed his neighborhood unit theory with a school at the center, very much in the manner of this suburban community.

The Architects Depart. In spite of the changing times, it would be wrong to assume that the architecture of the teens and twenties in this century lost all the momentum it had gained under geniuses like Hunt and Burnham. Remarkably accomplished architects carried on: Cass Gilbert, Bertram Goodhue, McKim, Post, and Arthur Brown, Jr. Architecture merely changed its emphasis somewhat, and the classical discipline was slow to fade. Nevertheless, architects no longer had control over all the urban planning: a gradually increasing number of other disciplines entered the picture as new problems arose.

In 1917 the Committee on Town Planning of the American Institute of Architects published its *City Planning Progress in the United States,* a survey of the entire country which effectively records the peak of architectural accomplishment in this field. Edward H. Bennett and his new partner, William E. Parsons (who later was to introduce the study of city planning to Yale University) had just rendered a plan for the Denver Civic Center, with its fountains by Lorado Taft. This formed the frontispiece of the book. But Bennett's planning reports were becoming increasingly "practical," and the foreword to the work in question also recognizes the fact that a movement had sprung up all over the country to plan the future growth of towns "in a businesslike way, and without waste." The Committee was "firmly convinced that city planning in America has been given to the 'City Beautiful' rather than the 'City Practical.' " All city planning, they thought, should start from a foundation of good business; "it must be something that will appeal to the business man, and to the manufacturer, as sane and reasonable." The mentality of Babbitt was thus catered to; and in removing the process from the realm of art, the architectural profession was losing its strongest right arm. In leafing through *City Planning Progress,* it is noteworthy how many of the artistic schemes were actually carried out, whereas in the City Practical era which followed we know that few got beyond the pages of a report. As Burnham had warned, they had no magic "to stir mens' blood," although they were often worthy documents full of pious hopes for "a better tomorrow for all the citizens."

The change can be traced in a list of planned towns prepared ten years later by John Nolen, President of the Nineteenth National Conference, for a retrospective speech given in Washington in May, 1927.[2] Nolen himself was a symptom of the new mood (he was a landscape architect and a "practical" planner), and his list is heavily weighted with architects until the time of the entry of the United States into World War I, after which engineers and various kinds of technical experts dominate. Nolen, too, talks about city-planning progress; but he notes that at the close of 1926 there was a total motor-vehicle registration of over twenty-two million cars, and he puts "how to relieve traffic congestion" first on his list of the needs of the next twenty years. He ends by quoting a new book, *Sticks and Stones,* by Lewis Mumford, urging mankind "to project fresh forms into which our energies must be freely poured." These forms were already appearing in Europe, devised by rebel architects for the age of glass and steel, and in the late twenties were beginning to attract attention in America. The aim of originality rather than any classical discipline would occupy the minds of the architectural profession by the time of World War II.

In the twenties, however, a strongly formalized plan as a setting for classical architecture could still command attention, and the period provided excellent examples which have stood the test of all critics. If modern architects of today could march in protest against the destruction of McKim, Mead, and White's Pennsylvania Station and the *New Yorker* magazine could campaign against the intrusion of advertising into Warren and Wetmore's Grand Central Concourse, there remain other monuments to the twenties which contrast just as strongly with the popular image of "The Jazz Age." There was until recently Park Avenue itself, a dignified model of the speculator's art in building urbane apartment houses. In Philadelphia the French planner Jacques Greber had cut through what is now known as the Benjamin Franklin Parkway, leading from the city hall to the new art museum in Fairmount Park. Both avenue and museum were begun in 1918. A larger triumph for Greber was his continuing work begun twenty years later on the planning of Ottawa, a

[2] *American Society of Planning Officials Newsletter* (Chicago, Illinois, 1966, 1967), Vol. 32, Nos. 6 and 12, Vol. 33, No. 1.

city which today owes much of its charm and distinctive features to his frequent visits over a long period of years.[3]

Then there was Washington, graced in the twenties with a new "quarter," the Triangle, where the work of Arthur Brown, Jr., perhaps America's most neglected important architect, found eloquent expression in the galleries and porches of the Interdepartmental Auditorium complex. Brown had designed the San Francisco City Hall, with what are probably the most magnificent interiors of any public building in America; together with the Veterans' Memorial Building and the San Francisco Opera House, the City Hall forms the focal point of a splendid civic center. It was Andrew Mellon who spurred the design of the Triangle, bringing Edward H. Bennett from Chicago to plan his last great triumph in the late 1920's. Delano and Aldrich designed the 12th Street Circle, only part of which was built, but which happily is included in a recent plan for the revival of Pennsylvania Avenue.

The building of the Triangle marks the end of the City Beautiful influence, and a noticeable gap occurs in monumental planning thereafter, lasting for a whole generation. Only today are there signs of a swinging back in taste to classical scale and proportion, which, because so few architects and planners have been trained to handle them, are being clumsily misinterpreted by designers of art and civic centers in the new movement for dignified settings. Mere size, as in the new Los Angeles Civic Center, proves to be no substitute for scale; and incised converging lines on the columns of the New York State Theater at Lincoln Center cannot make up for the lack of proportion in the columns themselves.

The Metro City. "A niggardly public life that made the citizen contemptuous of public officials is yielding to a dignified and beautiful public service that inspires love for the community and respect for its servants." So wrote Charles Zueblin in the

---

[3] The plan of Edward H. Bennett for Ottawa in 1915 was the basis for later developments in that capital city. Its illustrations were by Jules Guerin, the native artist who had made the perspectives for the 1909 plan of Chicago. They included bird's-eye views of the capital region and magnificent renderings of the public buildings, designed to show the desirability of height regulations.

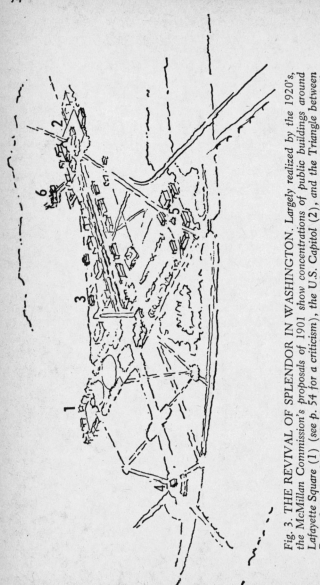

Fig. 3. THE REVIVAL OF SPLENDOR IN WASHINGTON. *Largely realized by the 1920's, the McMillan Commission's proposals of 1901 show concentrations of public buildings around Lafayette Square (1) (see p. 54 for a criticism), the U.S. Capitol (2), and the Triangle between Pennsylvania and Constitution Avenues (3) (see p. 73). The Lincoln Memorial (4) was built where proposed, and another suggested remembrance site (5) on a long vista from the White House, is now graced by the Jefferson Memorial. Burnham's Union Station is (6).*

second edition of his book, *American Municipal Progress,* published in 1916. While the reader may smile at the optimism of this statement, Zueblin was able to list an impressive list of civic improvements in which government was involved, all having taken place since 1902 when his book was first published. There were the first municipalized street railways, constructive provisions for health like milk stations and school nurses, the advent of policewomen, municipal reference libraries, the modern playground movement, the democratic art museum, the city manager, home rule for cities, direct legislation—and other novelties, which signified to the author "a greater advance than the whole nineteenth century compassed."

Although Zueblin does not mention zoning, just then about to be introduced, he does describe early attempts at metropolitan government in Boston and Los Angeles, noting some progress in amalgamating services. "Why not keep local governments for strictly local affairs?" he muses, "and have a popularly elected commission embracing all of the metropolitan functions?" Followers of this idea have been trying ever since to implement it; and only in the last few years have very limited successes been achieved in Miami, Florida, and Nashville, Tennessee. But even in Zueblin's day it was becoming apparent that a new kind of city was emerging. In 1922, N. S. B. Gras was the first to observe the established fact of a metropolitan economy, with a "hinterland" tied inexorably to the central city. This observation by an economic historian at a time when economic history was just becoming fashionable in the academies marks the beginning of studies of the urban economic structure.

Only a year before, a prototype of the autonomous authority had been set up as a method of dealing with a city which had sprawled over state boundaries. First envisaged as a means of improving out-of-date harbor facilities, the Port of New York Authority soon turned to highway-building, reaping financial rewards from bridge tolls, and, being tax-free, increasing the revenues of its bond-holders. Resisting efforts to use its revenues for New York's failing transportation system, the Authority has often been criticized for its conservative policies, especially by municipalities which stood to gain by building and operating the same facilities. Vastly successful, the Port Authority provided evidence that the cities had become too large to be governed in

a piecemeal fashion. With the state government loath to undertake planning, this new device was copied in a proliferation of
housing, parking, and even baseball stadium authorities; and,
as in the case of zoning, it was seized on as a substitute for comprehensive city development by planned coordination of activities. Later, the most famous municipal public servant of the
1930's and 1940's, Robert Moses, was to characterize these new
activities as "planning with limited objectives," and, as Chairman of the Triborough Bridge and Tunnel Authority, to resist
in his turn the demand for comprehensive planning of all of
New York's transportation system.

After New York's initial zoning experiment, this device swept
the country, catching on in a dozen California communities by
1922, finding favor in the Midwest and then in New England
states and Florida by 1925. An English observer said: "It was
as a means of strengthening the institution of private property
in the face of rapid and unsettling changes in the urban scene
that zoning won such remarkable acceptance in American communities." [4] Especially was it valuable in protecting the new
single-family suburban areas from encroachments by the city.
(*See Reading No. 31.*) This was the period in which city
dwellers began to move to the suburbs in large numbers, leaving
the central areas without the upper-class leadership they had
long retained. Wall Street in New York and State Street in Boston
might still claim the men by day, but their loyalties stayed with
their families in Bronxville and Brookline. Commuter railroads
helped, and a special fast train was run from Lake Forest to
the Chicago Loop in the mornings, for the businessmen and
bankers. Meanwhile, expensive shops had moved out to architect Howard Shaw's Old English shopping square in Lake Forest
itself, proving a great attraction for the wives to stay at home
and heralding the shopping center of today. The modern suburban shopping center is usually without any of the earlier charm
of Lake Forest's arcaded Market Square, or of the shopping
circle at Shaker Heights, a well-planned suburb of Cleveland.

It was a Chicago banker, Charles Dyer Norton, for some time
associated with the development of Burnham's plan for that city,

[4] John Delafons, *Land-Use Controls in the United States* (Cambridge,
Mass., 1962), p. 23.

who did most to urge a similar regional plan for New York.[5] Although Burnham worked on the earlier plan single-mindedly for years, refusing to accept any pay, Norton realized that he would need a committee and funds; and after several rebuffs persuaded the Russell Sage Foundation, which had financed Forest Hills Gardens, to underwrite the ten-year undertaking which started in the spring of 1922.

The technical studies were carried out by a team of planners, economists, and sociologists, led by Thomas Adams, an architect-engineer who had been connected with the Garden City movement in England. The studies were published in eight volumes and the plans described in two more. The region in 1925 had a resident population of 9,900,000 people, living in about 500 municipal areas. Four years after the plan was published, Adams pointed with pride to the fact that 109 of these areas had acquired official planning boards; and there were 257 unofficial planning councils. Two hundred seventy-three zoning ordinances were in effect and thirty-one in preparation. More directly, the plan influenced the region's highway and parkway system, which Adams did not live to see completed. Many of the major parkways, which Robert Moses justifiably claimed as his creations, were originally traced in the transportation plan. In Volume 7, Clarence Perry discussed his neighborhood unit plan, in which he proposed that the unit of population be limited to a number which could be served by one school, thus advocating the planning of school-centered communities, a theory now being questioned in some educational and housing circles. Perhaps the plan's most lasting effect can be found in the continuing activities of the Regional Plan Association, a nonprofit organization devoted to research and recommendations concerning the region's future, which has been directed for some years past by C. McKim Norton, son of the man who envisaged the problems the region would face in the future. (*See Reading No. 32.*)

[5] C. McKim Norton writes: "My father was a member of the Commercial Club which I believe helped to spark Chicago's first plan. They were all very much stimulated by the World's Fair. The fact that Charles F. McKim was my mother's uncle probably had something to do with my parents' involvement in the Fair. I know my father was a friend of Daniel Burnham's." (From a letter to the author, March 15, 1967.)

The New York Regional Survey and Plan was a bold stab at the task of metropolitan development along orderly lines, and an important influence. Criticized by members of a newly-formed Regional Planning Association of America, an informal organization which included Lewis Mumford, Henry Wright, and Clarence Stein, it was termed by them not true regional planning and merely an extension of city planning to a wider area, based on expediency and the immediately practicable. These objections ignored the Plan's quest for livability in the giant region's surroundings, an approach which was advanced for its day. When these same critics made a demonstration of their own in 1928, their ideal town of Radburn, billed as "A Town for the Motor Age," failed for lack of financial support and an apparent inability to attract industry. Two of the "super-blocks" designed to separate automobile and pedestrian traffic were built before the Wall Street crash, and have found favor with those who enjoy the many social activities centered on the Grange and who commute to the big city twelve miles away in their working hours.

Shapes of Democracy. If zoning and other land-use controls were being accepted as a means of preventing intrusions into enclaves of gracious suburban living, these newly developed aspects of the police power were scarcely changing the face of the city in any recognizable way. In fact, the only major city to hold out against zoning, Houston, Texas, today scarcely looks any different from other places of its size. There was, however, something new on the city skyline: the tower-form skyscraper.

The earlier "tall-buildings" (described in Chapter 4) often had elaborately designed fronts facing the street, leaving the backs and sides gaunt and harsh, even though they were perfectly visible from the side streets. Buildings of this nature dominated the city center of 1910. Chance governed their placing, and "all showed the terrific expanses of chaotic, wasted roof surfaces, disfigured with scuttles and water-tanks," as Talbot Hamlin described them in the 1920's. A typical example is the Taft Hotel in New Haven, Connecticut, well-known to generations of football enthusiasts, which for years alone dominated the New Haven skyline, until the Collegiate Gothic Harkness Tower was built for Yale University by the architect James Gamble Rogers.

In New York, the Metropolitan Life Insurance Company's tower by Napoleon le Brun and Sons (1906) had broken this pattern; but that city's significant breakthrough came in 1911-1913 with the Woolworth Building by Cass Gilbert (1859-1934), one of this period's most brilliant architects. Admired largely because it was the then-tallest building in the world, its delicate pencil-pointing of the skyline and its lacelike Gothic decoration, covering the whole building, achieved a greater triumph and outshone anything that Louis Sullivan had been able to bring to the esthetic form of the tall building. Both Gilbert and Bertram Goodhue, architects of classical state capitols, occasionally played with the Gothic; but it is noteworthy that Goodhue turned to the classic again in his great tower for the Nebraska State Capitol, visible for miles across the northwestern plains. The Woolworth tower is more romantic in feeling, with its wealth of terracotta tracery; yet it is also an expression of the construction, showing the breaks for the floors of mechanical equipment, something that early modern architects were trying to achieve in quite a different way. It was also self-washing, a convenience which recent glass-clad slab-towers have not been able to introduce.

Here was America's greatest contribution to world architecture. Its companions, the later Tribune Tower and a host of other tower-form skyscrapers in Chicago as well as many other cities, large and small, bring home to us the fact well-recognized in Europe that all through the twenties and culminating in the building of the Empire State tower in 1930, the United States led the world in architectural excellence.

Meanwhile, a relatively-unobserved phenomenon was occurring on the West Coast, obscured perhaps by the popular glamor and publicity surrounding some of its immigrants, the New York actors and Chicago ice-cream parlor waitresses who had become movie stars. Los Angeles was changing from a health resort and center of the citrus trade into a major manufacturing center and port, but the statistic that fascinated some demographers had to do with population growth. Although in 1903 a law could still be passed forbidding the driving of more than 2000 sheep down Hollywood Boulevard at any one time, the local population had already edged past the 100,000 mark. With Los Angeles as a magnet, the fourteen southernmost counties of California have since doubled in population every twenty years, until, as of 1965, they had an estimated population of 12,110,000 people, moving

ahead of two large states, Illinois and Pennsylvania, in total
number of inhabitants.

The rapidity of this growth (at times five to six times as fast
as the United States as a whole) is no longer merely a matter
of Chamber of Commerce boasting, and is being "viewed with
alarm" by those who see too much dependence on the local
aircraft industry itself, which is now experimenting with the
manufacture of surface transportation vehicles and other side-
lines. Even in the late twenties the haphazard growth of Los
Angeles had given rise to popular images of "the city without
a center" (*see Reading No. 33*) and a commuter's nightmare.
(The typical Los Angeleno still spends one hour, 36 minutes
in travel time, to and from work.) But before the Great Depression of the 1930's it was hard to believe that growth was anything but a blessing in American city life; and the fact that the
brave new tall buildings, which somehow expressed this blessing
and had been called by Walt Whitman "shapes of democracy,"
would soon come to be derided as symbols of the folly of Wall
Street, would have been credited by only a discerning few.

CHAPTER 7

The American City in Trouble

Back to the Land.   The last monumental tower-form skyscraper was a beacon on the New York skyline, but like many
monuments it remained at first impressive and empty. For ten
years the Empire State Building stood as a reminder of another
age, desperately seeking tenants, filling only gradually and reaching capacity during World War II, when the federal Office of
Price Administration took over several of the upper floors.

Before March, 1933 (the beginning of the Hundred Days),
the nation was in a state of shock and near-panic. It was all
very well for John D. Rockefeller, when asked by reporters
what he was doing in the Depression, to reply calmly, "My son
and I are buying Common"; but the country needed more assur-
ance than that. The first Roosevelt administration introduced a
host of remedies in that first March-to-June session of Congress.

In setting out to lick the prevailing slump, the New Deal was remarkably successful with the problems of the farmers, but did not fare so well with the cities. (*See Reading No. 34.*)

Henry Wallace was convinced that when former civilizations had fallen it was because they had failed to maintain a balance between city and country. Noting with the Progressives that the city had come to dominate American life, he set out to restore the balance. As Secretary of Agriculture, and with the help of the able Assistant Secretary, Rexford Tugwell, his Department initiated price supports, the retirement of marginal land, and subsidies to stimulate export. In spite of the dustbowl tragedy and other setbacks, farm recovery began to move faster than income and employment elsewhere. Later, Tugwell, as head of the Resettlement Administration, was able to experiment with satellite cities, taking his cue from Ebenezer Howard. As Howard's Garden City movement had done, Tugwell wanted to go outside the central cities, find land at agricultural prices, build new towns, and move people out to them. Then, remarkably like Howard's suggested plan for London in the 1890's, he would "go back to the cities, tear down whole slums and make parks of them." This last he was not able to do, but three Greenbelt Towns did emerge as demonstrations of the theory. President Roosevelt thought the cost too high and the location of the Resettlement projects too arbitrary for them to become self-supporting. Indeed, the three Greenbelt towns, located near Washington, Milwaukee, and Cincinnati, are now suburban to those cities. Arthur M. Schlesinger suggests in *The Coming of the New Deal* that Tugwell may actually havce been anticipating later suburban waves; if so, his settlements were hardly paving the way for "a new type of civilization."

The metropolitan centers found themselves in 1933 with half-completed projects and massive unemployment. The Triborough Bridge had to be completed by means of a Public Works Administration loan. Federal funds were also needed for the West Side Improvement in New York. What with highways, tunnels, and bridges, by 1935 almost three-fifths of all public expenditures for new public construction came from Washington. Previously the average had been one-twelfth.

It is to be noted that many of these public-works projects facilitated the use of the automobile; although schools, sewage plants, and hospitals also benefited from PWA funds. Congressional support for public housing, however, did not come until 1937 and under pressure from labor unions and the construction industry, which was only slowly recovering from the Depression. In that year the Wagner-Steagall Act established the United States Housing Authority. At long last, and a whole generation after most countries of Europe, the nation had acknowledged its responsibility for low-income family shelter. Even so, many thought the pace too slow for the need, since by 1940 only about 160,000 dwelling units were made available to the poor. During World War II, however, the Authority, together with Jesse Jones' creation, the Federal Housing Administration, were to prove essential instruments in alleviating overcrowded conditions in shipbuilding centers and war-manufacturing areas of the country.

It was thus that in attempting to revive the economy, the way was "paved" for the rapid decentralization of the cities after 1935. Other developments helped—the shorter workweek, government mortgage guarantees—but the suburbanization of American life could not have taken the form it did without society's indirect subsidization of the automobile industry.

A by-product of the Public Works Administration made history by being created at all. This was the National Planning Board, established in 1933, which eventually came to be called the National Resources Planning Board until its demise during the war. Roosevelt felt it was necessary to put the physical development of the country on a planned basis, and wanted a permanent, long-range planning commission which could lay out a far-seeing program for national development. In spite of the opponents of planning—Congressman Joe Martin of Massachusetts had called the TVA "a copy of one of the Soviet dreams," and Everett M. Dirksen of Illinois thought that the development of power and fertilizer in that locality could be "of no general good"—the President with Senator Norris's help in the Senate had succeeded in getting river basin resource-planning through the Congress; and although the legislators would not go along with a later Seven TVA's Bill to extend the principle to other parts of the country, most of the doubting voices were silenced when TVA proved of inestimable value to the war effort after 1942.

Harold Ickes, however, made sure that the Board remained

only an advisory committee when its executive officer, Charles W. Eliot II, drew up a plan to make it an independent agency. As Secretary of the Interior, Ickes liked to sail a very tight ship. In spite of its lack of power, however, the National Resources Planning Board had good advisers in men like Frederick A. Delano, the President's uncle, and Charles E. Merriam, who had experience in Chicago politics. An excellent series of reports were produced, including such outstanding works as *Farm Tenancy* and *The Future of the Great Plains*. The public was educated in the values of planning, and in part of its 1934 Report the Board produced *A Plan for Planning*, which remains one of the most important documents ever published in that field. State planning, which Roosevelt had pushed hard as Governor of New York, received help and encouragement at the same time.

In its relation to the cities, the National Resources Planning Board has a mixed record. Many of the studies it supported helped to spur the housing and public-works aspect of the New Deal's history. Its Urbanism Committee's *Our Cities: Their Role in the National Economy* was another pioneering document, pointing out to the nation how chaotically organized were the governments of urban areas. But the record of the Local Planning Committee was one of continuous controversy, and it did not last. Professor George S. Duggar of the University of Pittsburgh, who worked for the Board, suggests that it did not settle the matter of the best method for doing local planning. Further, it can be said in the light of developments since that day that the Board may have been short-sighted in its approach to the developing urban regions. It seemed to favor the Mumford-Stein approach to the methods of regional planning. "To construct regions which would adhere to cities . . . is to place the emphasis on one factor rather than the total region," pronounced the Board in 1935, echoing Mumford's attack on the Regional Plan of New York as a "purely arbitrary concept, based upon future possibilities of transportation and past facts of city growth." (*See Reading No. 35.*)

"A Few Choice Flowers." The National Resources Planning Board made America aware of its urban blight, and the Roosevelt administration chose to correct this situation in part by creating new housing. When New York's pugnacious and much-loved Mayor La Guardia opened development-after-public-development on the East Side, stretching from Brooklyn Bridge up into Harlem, he was wont to beam proudly at the dedication, referring to "my latest project." It was, however, Uncle Sam who made them possible. Later, when Robert Moses persuaded the Metropolitan Life Insurance Company to build "Stuyvesant Town" just above 14th Street, it was the city's turn to be generous. Although the project was controversial, La Guardia backed it, describing the thirteen-story buildings as being in "a delightful residential community with trees and parks." The city gave it eleven acres of land free of charge (the discontinued streets in the superblock) and tax exemption over a period of years amounting to some $25,000,000. When the public discovered that this private project nearly trebled the net density of the area and that its policy was to exclude Negroes, there were loud cries of anger. Other means had to be found to encourage private enterprise to take part thereafter in slum clearance and rehabilitation. Meanwhile, the new urban redevelopment laws (New York's came into being in 1942) left the slum problem unsolved.

From a design standard, a few projects of the war years are outstanding. Baldwin Hills Village, Los Angeles (Federal Housing Administration), returned to a symmetrical, classical plan and was immediately acclaimed. Linda Vista, also in California, introduced the idea of a shopping center surrounding a park. Otherwise, the New Deal had pioneered in creating new public buildings in cities and towns all over the United States. What is more, it had employed artists to decorate them.

The Public Works Administration had spent over $7 billion under Harold Ickes' careful scrutiny. Ickes did much to preserve the national heritage in national parks and historic buildings, which he was wont to call "shrines." But the New Deal was built on the idea of providing employment; and the much-maligned Works Progress Administration, under the aegis of Harry Hopkins, spent $10.5 billion between 1935 and 1942, employing millions of people.

Among these were over 3,600 artists, who, under the Public Works of Art Project, were commissioned to paint murals in the new post offices and courthouses. Edward Bruce, the corporation lawyer-turned-artist, organized this first federal subsidy of mural artists, many of whom were saved from dire poverty by this program. Bruce pointed out that it did more. The program proved, he thought, that the artist was not a solitary worker, aiming to please a small minority of specialists. The people were expressing a real interest in the artists' achievements. Leafing through the volume of these public works of art one comes across names that have since become famous and others that have been forgotten.[1] Art patronage must of necessity become prodigal and as the architectural historian Louis Hautecoeur put it: "It takes many dead leaves to create the soil needed to bring forth a few choice flowers." (*See Readings Nos. 36 and 37.*)

The Suburbanization of American Life. In spite of its innovations, like the public-housing program, employment of artists in public programs, and experimental new towns, the New Deal did not solve the problems of the cities. Its "back-to-the-land" approach got rid of most of the "Hoovervilles" that had sprung up in rural areas, and the tar-paper shacks that served for country residences in the Depression have almost all disappeared, except in Appalachia and the Deep South. But soon another form of blight began to appear along the same country roads and three-lane highways. This time it was commercial in nature. The selling of automobiles, shoes, clothing, and groceries in the new commercial strips in suburbia and even further out in the urban-rural fringe dealt further blows at the city, which had hitherto drawn all the shoppers to its central business district. Especially hard hit were the shopkeepers of small towns, who found it impossible to compete with the prices and attractions of the outlying shopping centers.

The postwar wave of suburban development had been predicted, but it was not foreseen by the big-city mayors or their advisers. In fact, for years it went unremarked because it did not seem remarkable. "Scatteration" of settlement had always been a part of American life. When the historical painter John Singleton Copley in 1771 rode from Boston to New York, noticing that during the whole journey "you scarcely lose sight of an house," he was merely recording the fact that the New England township was not a European cluster of habitations but a spread-out network of farms and dwelling-houses.

When H. G. Wells predicted in 1902 that a new form of settlement pattern which he called "the urban region" would

[1] Edward Bruce and Forbes Watson, *Art in Federal Buildings* (Washington, 1936). Vol. I. "Mural Design."

develop, especially in the United States, he was only fifty years
ahead of the event. In the new urban regions, said Wells, a
citizen of Philadelphia would feel quite at home in Albany and
vice versa, because the settlement pattern would be the same
and communications immeasurably speeded up. After World
War II the linkages were made. Trucks came up from Texas
with produce that the urbanized states of the seaboard and the
north-central areas of the country could no longer grow. Execu-
tives travelled by an expanded airline network from Chicago
and California to head offices in the East. Pipelines brought oil
and natural gas from South to North. Expressways made it
easier to live away from the city yet not be isolated from it.
They also encouraged cross-commuting, so that a factory worker
could live in New Jersey and work in an aircraft plant on Long
Island, driving twice across Manhattan in one day.

The phenomenon was not new, yet as late as the 1920's it
could still be said that the central cities dominated all phases
of the American culture. This was no longer so. While the talking
pictures were killing big-city vaudeville, other changes were taking place. Although the centers were still powerful magnets,
many of them were beginning to lose population; and it was now
the suburbs that conditioned not only people's lives but their
thoughts and the communications media as well. Magazines with
a national circulation became suburban-oriented; humor on radio
and television revolved around the problems of suburban living.
Although there *were* problems—long commuting hours for the
men, women of child-bearing age tied more tightly to the home,
rising taxes combined with a lack of public services, and so on—
there were vast compensations. A shorter working week and the
growth of labor unions provided more leisure time coupled with
job security. The movement of industry to the urban-rural fringe
provided a choice of employment. There was the blessing of
privacy, not only within the four walls of one's Federal Housing
Administration mortgage-guaranteed home, but outside on the
much larger lot that the outer reaches of urbanization now af-
forded, and where father could build his boat in the backyard
while the children splashed in their plastic pool. Suburban shopping centers remained open in the evenings, so that the whole
family could go, or mother could take the older children while
father remained home with the baby.

This spread-out form of living suggested to many Americans that there was no other settlement pattern which could suit their way of life so well. True, conservationists deplored the way the land was disappearing before the bulldozer, and planners warned of problems of communication and ill-advised fringe development. (Monroe County, New York, by introducing piped water along its county roads, gave farmers the opportunity to sell off their frontage lots, so that a stringlike residential settlement pattern one lot deep began to appear in formerly rural areas.) But generally speaking, few were concerned about altering the way of life or revolutionizing the building pattern. The sociologist Robert C. Wood, who later became an official of the federal Department of Housing and Urban Development, saw no drastic changes in view. "We know of no other time," he observed, "when a revolution took place when the existing system was solidly established, and its citizens, as they understood the goals of their domestic society, content." [2]

Citizens without Hope.   Those who sought an Elysium in the former Long Island potato fields or the woods of Rockland County, New York, were escaping from a city which had always known slums, but which had deteriorated badly during World War II and had developed social problems of a magnitude quite unforeseen by the early housing reform movement. The remedy to be applied this time was urban redevelopment and renewal, which, after 1949, supplied federal funds for land clearance and acquisition in residential and commercial districts.

The 1811 plan had laid out a pattern for the northern part of Manhattan Island, while the 1916 zoning ordinance had fixed the avenues as commercial and the side streets as residential. At the time of the 1811 Commissioners' plan, President Timothy Dwight of Yale College noted that Harlem contained about eighty houses, "most of them neat; and among them several country seats belonging to citizens of New York; together with a church of the Dutch communion." [3] In 1850 there were over 1,500 houses and it took an hour-and-a-half to get to the business

---

[2] Robert C. Wood, "The Political Economy of the Future," in *City and Suburb,* Benjamin Chinitz (ed.), (Prentice-Hall, Englewood Cliffs, N.J., 1964), p. 176.

[3] Timothy Dwight, *Travels: In New England and New York* III, p. 484.

district of New York by horse car or steamer. By 1890 Harlem was a pleasant residential district of the wealthy and the less well-to-do, with shops that catered to the carriage trade and Oscar Hammerstein's Opera House, in which warbled the greatest divas of the day. This period was important for the future of Harlem, accounting for the little-noticed phenomenon that its structures today are in many cases well-built and still service-able, and that it has a comparatively low skyline, admitting plenty of light and air into side-streets which further down the island have become canyons of tall buildings.

In 1900 the first Negro residents appeared at 134th Street, and by 1914 the major influx began, while the Italian in-migration stopped. Negroes had already lived in several parts of New York, and in George Washington's day had been tavern and restaurant owners, as well as domestic servants living in dilapidated hous-ing, although not the "shanty towns" of the Germans and Irish. In 1850 the Negro district was on the fringes of Washington Square, and in 1885 in the Chelsea district; by 1895 there were three main "integrated" Negro areas: in the Williamsburg district of Brooklyn, in the West 50's (centered about 53rd Street), and in the West 60's (San Juan Hill). Because of resi-dential development in the 1880's, housing in Harlem was more modern and sunnier than any available at the turn of the century; and shrewd white businessmen used fear of the Negro to stam-pede whole blocks into selling at very low prices.

The greatest age of Harlem began in 1920, when Negroes bought houses with money earned during the war; and although banks did not lend money to Negroes, business and entertainment grew along the commercially-zoned avenues. By 1930 Harlem held 65 percent of all Negroes in New York City and was the center of the North American Negro world. Almost every major Negro institution moved there. Writers, musicians, and poets like Langston Hughes made Harlem a mecca for intellectuals. But although it has gained in population (and consequent overcrowd-ing), Harlem no longer holds the place it did in Negro life. Although it now contains over a quarter of a million people and 30 percent of the city's Negroes, Central Harlem has no public high school. It has the highest infant mortality rate in the city. Twelve public-housing projects have not prevented the highest crime rate in the city from being found there. In spite of the fact that Harlem's gross product is greater than that of any West African country, only ½ of 1 percent of its residents are home owners. Many Negroes have moved to the interior suburbs of Brooklyn, the Bronx, and Queens.

Impossible pressures have bred resentment and riots. The governmental remedies of urban renewal and anti-poverty programs have not worked. Indeed, the former has been criticized for aggravating the situation: between 1950 and 1957 fully half the residents of cleared dwellings in New York City were Negro, while only 5 percent of the new construction was occupied by nonwhites.

There are some who say that the Negro ghetto is a social phenomenon which has come to stay, and that the Negro would just as soon live in the Harlems of the United States if he could get a job and a better education for his children. There are some who say that only when Negroes are accepted on a kinship basis by nonwhites will segregation be a thing of the past. There are some who say the Negro problem is a national problem which will only be solved in economic terms. If so, the cities are now more of a national phenomenon than ever, since Negroes count for more than half the total population in cities like Washington, D.C. Lily-white suburbs help to keep the Negroes in the central cities, where too often a spirit of hopelessness prevails and youth gangs roam the streets. At all events, by the mid-twentieth century the cities of America were in the gravest trouble of their chequered history, and grappling with their social problems began to take priority over physical rebuilding for the first time in their two-and-one-half centuries of growth.

The Return of the Picturesque.   The National Gallery of Art in Washington and the Empire State Building were the last important monuments repectively of the classical revival and the age of the tower-form skyscraper. These were succeeded by an anti-classical phase of architecture characterized by the office or apartment house slab, often of curtain-wall construction with sides of glass. It was a sign of the postwar times that when a new state office building or a city hall was built, as in Chicago, that the nonmonumental slab form was used for these ceremonial buildings, just as it was used for banks and business offices. No longer could one pick out a civic center or library by its decorative appearance; these, as was the case with other public buildings, seemed to have adopted the architectural manners of the business world.

The reasons for this change in taste were due less to technology itself than to fascination on the part of architects and architecture with the idea of technology. New art movements like Futurism during World War I had been enchanted by the development of the machine. Adolf Loos, the Austrian Secessionist, had preached the abolition of ornament. German architects of the 1920's had proclaimed an age of glass in architecture. Some of them came to the United States in this period, spreading a rationalist doctrine into the schools, the first courses in what came to be called "modern" architecture being given by the elder Saarinen at the University of Michigan in the early thirties. The Swiss designer Le Corbusier who became the "architect's architect" of the period, announced that a house was a machine for living.

Not that all the inspiration came from abroad. Albert Kahn, the largely self-taught architect from Detroit, had been designing reinforced concrete factories with walls of glass since 1905. And when Adolf Loos' trainee, Richard Neutra, arrived in California in 1925 to start building his constructivist houses, he found that his fellow Austrian, R. M. Schindler, was already there, having collaborated with Frank Lloyd Wright on the Barnsdall House in Los Angeles. Well before that period the California architects Greene and Greene and Irving Gill had shown examples of picturesque composition and elimination of ornament in their reworking of the California bungalow and introduction of the Sullivanian private house respectively.

For some artists and architects the tradition of Picturesque Secessionism never died. Sullivan lived on, tragically unhappy, while his disciple Frank Lloyd Wright built suburban houses in Oak Park, Illinois, which, after a brief flirtation with classicism, became more and more imbued with picturesque originality. Wright had been enormously impressed with the rationalism of Viollet-le-Duc. He pressed the *Discourses* of the French restorer into his son's hands, telling him that therein was all the architecture he would ever need to know; adding, characteristically, "The rest you can learn from me." And while he would never have admitted that Le Corbusier, domiciled in France, had a claim higher than his own in the development of modern architecture, he may have observed on seeing *Vers une Architecture,*

Le Corbusier's testament of 1923, that the author's term "functionism" was merely an updating of the "honesty-of-construction" doctrine that Viollet-le-Duc had avowed in the 1860's. Certainly Wright's term "organic architecture" comes out of Viollet-le-Duc's pages.

Significantly, a cause to which both Wright and Le Corbusier subscribed in the 1930's was the rebuilding of cities. In both cases the solution was drastic. It was nothing less than a clean sweep and a rebuilding in the form of a low-density agrarian town or a vertical garden city of low coverage. While Wright railed against bankers, Le Corbusier called for reform of finance capitalism, both centering their attacks on the dominance of city life. While this was architectonic Utopianism born of frustration and personal disillusion with society, Broadacre City and the Ville Radieuse gained wide publicity. In the United States, models were shown at the Museum of Modern Art in New York, an institution supported by that branch of the Rockefeller family interested in "advanced" art from the School of Paris. Students flocked to this institution to hear pundits like Lewis Mumford hurl barbs at the condition of man; and when in 1937 the Harvard School of Design opened its doors to Walter Gropius and Marcel Breuer, the stage was set for a whole generation of modern architects. These teachers had been at the Bauhaus, a German rationalist institution which had discovered structural principles in all the arts: the design of a chair or a teapot went through the same process as that of a house or a city; building was sculpture, and was related to abstract painting. So excited were American architects by the Bauhaus principles that they became impatient with the grim reality of their own environment and believed that the world could be reformed by design. An apocryphal story told by a former head of the American Academy in Rome concerns his showing the well-known view over the city from its terrace to a Fellow fresh from the Harvard architectural school. The young man looked at all this beauty sadly. Shaking his head, he observed: "What a pity it all has to come down!" (*See Reading No. 38.*)

This extreme view of redevelopment cannot be said to have influenced the federal government in funding the rebuilding of cities after the Housing Act of 1949 (*see Reading No. 39*), especially since most architects were working in suburban areas.

But when a few modern architects succeeded in obtaining large commissions, some of their clients also became interested in cleared and cleaned sites. Such clients could be found on the building committees of banks, insurance companies, and hotel corporations; the architect still dealt with individuals on the building committees of these institutions, but these individuals had scarcely the force or knowledge of a J. P. Morgan. They wanted bland, noncontroversial advertisements in the form of buildings. The slab was eminently suitable for this purpose, and after Lever House on Park Avenue by Skidmore, Owings, and Merrill set the standard, this was the accepted style. Park Avenue above Grand Central Station was rebuilt in the next fifteen years, and dwarfed by a giant slab over the terminal's platforms for which Walter Gropius was hired as consultant. Whatever the companies gained in the way of publicity, such activities were no advertisement for city planning.

Between the frenzy of activity in Manhatan to build office buildings for headquarters of international corporations and the acres of empty cleared slums that resulted from much of urban renewal there was a wasteland of urban streets and buildings crying out for the attention of planners. Raymond Vernon dubbed these the "grey areas" in his restudy of New York for the Regional Plan Association, an organization which had continued to press for metropolitan planning through all the years following its publication of the monumental Plan of New York in 1929.

The postwar period was marked by activity in functional planning rather than centralized planning; that is, single-purpose public and private works by agencies, autonomous authorities, and institutions. The most noticeable innovations were the freeways. These were built by state highway departments with federal funds, granted by the Congress for an interstate system linking the great cities for defense purposes. The American public took to them like ducks to water, and, since they ran through urban areas as well as rural, found them as convenient for local trips as for long distance vacation travel. The trucking industry profited as well. Los Angeles, which for long had depended largely on the automobile for transportation became the first automotive city of the country, although scarcely a week went by without some mention of the need for rapid-transit facilities in the press.

Finally, in 1965, its rival for state metropolitan laurels, San Francisco, passed a bond issue for a new form of public transportation which it was hoped would link the central city with its ever-growing suburbs; and a fresh look at the transportation system of the nation's cities began to be demanded by Congress and public alike.

CHAPTER 8

"Twenty and Thirty and Forty Years On"

Aims and Goals. The new Interstate Highway System, linking up the already-expanded centers of urban population, contributed mightily to the forces deciding where Americans would live in the 1960's and the foreseeable future. With almost three million people being added yearly to the population, 82 percent of this increase was to be found in the suburban parts of metropolitan areas.

Discontent with the cities, however, was not to be found so much among the people who lived out in the urban counties "in spacious middle-income bungalows for white people only," as Adam Clayton Powell, the congressman from Harlem, put it, as among those who were left behind. Forty-four percent of all Negroes lived in substandard housing while only 13 percent of all white people did so; and when new housing was provided in the central cities for Negroes, Powell angrily termed it "segregated high-rise concentration camps for black people." And, in fact, by the mid-1960's, less public housing for low-income groups was being constructed. Charles Abrams, the New York housing expert, observed that the program was becoming a diminished appendage to the urban renewal programs. With the median family income of just under $4,000, Negroes could scarcely afford to rent any other new construction. They were thus forced into tenements and converted brownstones; and although the rent strike in New York became a useful weapon against exploitation, many Negroes paid too large a proportion of their income in rent. In the black sections of Harlem, where over 50 percent of the housing was substandard, the incidence of crime was over six times the city's average and dope addiction over fifteen times as prevalent.[1]

It was no wonder, thought Raymond Vernon, a professor in the Harvard Business School, that the standard prescriptions for American urban areas no longer seemed to serve. According to this authority, who, in the early 1960's made an exhaustive study of New York's metropolitan region, these prescriptions were: better mass transit to the central city, more low-cost housing in the central city, and tighter zoning in the suburbs.

Vernon proposed a fourth prescription, turning largely upon commercial renewal, which was already much in favor among businessmen in the retail trades. Why not, he suggested, try to reverse the process of decentralization by sending the poor out to the suburbs and bringing the élite back to the center? (In Vernon's terms the élite meant an income classification somewhat broader than that of fashionable society.) The prescription ran thus: Use commercial redevelopment to revivify the downtown business center; build apartments for the élite in the old slum areas outside it; and, with the help of rent subsidies and the money formerly spent for public housing in the cities, assist the poor to move out to suburban areas where their factory jobs would be nearby. Although he realized that this suggestion might conjure up visions of "a Golden Ghetto set down in surrounding squalor," Vernon thought that there was no alternative for keeping the middle-income groups in his rehabilitated grey areas. Otherwise, he saw a segregated city, with only the poor occupying its heart.[2]

Vernon's book, like so much of the planning literature of the mid-1960's, is revealing for its attitude toward preferred income groups. Persuasive as his solution may be, it gives the poor no choice. In some cities the poor have already been moved three times to make way for redevelopment projects, and, in at least a few, have been aided by the local administration in seeking homes in nearby communities! This common attitude, which by 1960 had already given urban renewal a bad name in neighborhood circles,

[1] Alexander Garvin, "Harlem, N.Y.: Fabulous Magnet and National Crisis," in *World Order*, Vol. 2, No. 2, December 1967.

[2] Raymond Vernon, *The Myth and Reality of Our Urban Problems* (Cambridge, Mass., 1966), pp. 67-91.

produced a counterrevolution in poor districts such as Woodlawn, next door to the University of Chicago, and The Hill, in New Haven, Connecticut, which had become overcrowded as a result of "Negro removal." Local protest movements tended to stall plans for renewal in these areas; and many people, in and out of the poverty class, began to call for an end to urban renewal as practiced by local government, unless it was willing to consider the poor as clients.

This revolt, spurred on by urban activists like Jane Jacobs, who prevented New York's renewal of West Greenwich Village, stirred Washington's new federal Department of Housing and Urban Development to initiate a Model Cities program, in which communities could get more urban-renewal funds if they could demonstrate a meshing of their renewal, welfare, anti-poverty, and other federally-financed programs. Whatever the program was to prove otherwise, it was at least a tacit admission that physical planning needed social planning behind it, and an end to the era of slum clearance as a panacea for city improvement.

Restudying the Past. In the process of playing their expensive game of musical chairs for increased revenues, the cities found themselves at war with another group of their inhabitants, the intellectuals and the rich. If urban renewal had brought together Democratic mayors and largely Republican Chambers of Commerce, threatened invasions of upper-income neighborhoods and destruction of historic buildings united college professors and retired businessmen and their wives in attacking highway plans that took park-land or renewal plans which destroyed valuable evidence of a living past. In the process, Save-the-Park committees and Historic Preservation Trusts discovered that, besides the ignorance and venality of local and state administrations, destruction of cherished buildings and sites was being blithely undertaken by their own favorite institutions: the universities, the churches, and the country clubs. All were either moving or expanding, and as one university president put it, "My institution must put education of new generations before the preservation of the monuments of the past," apparently not perceiving any relationship between the two concepts. (*See Reading No. 40.*)

New values, however, were being placed on these monuments, and many a president and corporation were surprised by the way people began to regard what otherwise might be considered rather shaky structures standing in the path of progress. Just as the slums were being reconsidered as perhaps worthy of rehabilitation rather than hostages to the bulldozer's greedy maw, wealthy Trinity Church in New York was reexamining its building policy in the light of that city's new Landmarks Commission's designation of several of its properties as part of the cultural patrimony of the nation. Several states by the 1960's had enabling legislation permitting their communities to establish historic districts, in which owners could not alter or demolish their buildings without approval. The most notable of these districts were Beacon Hill in Boston, the historic district of Nantucket, the Stockade district of Schenectady, and Historic Georgetown in the nation's capital; but there were historic districts, large and small, in dozens of cities and towns. They were always the result of local pressures, frequently aided by the expertise and publicity given by the National Trust for Historic Preservation, a private organization chartered by act of Congress in 1947. In 1966, a National Historic Preservation Act was passed, acknowledging that government funding of preservation would help the private efforts of individuals and groups; at the same time the Demonstration Cities bill provided means to retain historic structures in urban renewal districts.

By the mid-1960's federal funds were also available for open space acquisition and beautification of streets and squares. Something fundamental was missing, however, from attempts by municipalities to improve their amenities and appearance, in lieu of which the attempts to screen automobile-wrecking yards and remove billboards appeared as elementary cosmetics. This was the seeming inability to develop workable formulae for rehabilitation of old buildings, which few big builders would touch but which were desperately needed in the new climate of helping the poor to help themselves. Small-scale and early attempts to make run-down but structurally sound dwellings habitable again invariably carried a high price tag. Those who proved that it was cheaper to rehabilitate than to build anew were seldom heard from, although one could already see dozens of row houses in downtown Philadelphia converted by small firms of private developers where the fact had been established.

With hopeful signs of many more people becoming interested in historic preservation, preservation not only of buildings having strictly historical associations but of architecturally interesting structures as well, it remained for society to find new ways of incorporating them into the living conditions that would make the city tolerable for all income groups. Certainly the "slash-and-cut" approach would have to be replaced with a skill approaching that of the plastic surgeon before decent neighborhoods of character and architectural interest could be achieved on any scale.

The Form of the City. Having survived many vicissitudes since its birth a hundred years before, the modern American city now stands in danger of dismemberment. This is partly a result of the "project" approach favored by urban-renewal bureaucracy, by single-function agencies of the states (such as the highway departments), by expansion plans of institutions that exclude whole groups of citizens, and most drastically when all three power groups combine forces to push through a project in which federal grants, loans, tax remission, or other rewards are forthcoming. The results can be: a downtown center remade in the image of a suburban shopping mall, surrounded by freeways and parking lots; a series of housing projects between urban arterials and the railroads, as in Chicago, where low-income housing is in effect a new form of segregation for deprived Negroes; an urban university expanding into a slum area and using renewal funds to cut itself off from the poor by a ring road and parking garages; frequent attempts to invade city parks with freeways, as in Shaker Heights, Ohio, or to cut cities off from their waterfronts, as in the Vieux Carré in New Orleans; the separating-off of cultural facilities in new centers, as in dozens of little Lincoln Centers in cities all over the country; and many other examples of one-group or one-function isolates.

Those who could remember the city in which all classes mingled together in the streets and lived in comparative harmony cheek by jowl, were able to compare the midcentury city unfavorably with urban America of the 1920's. If public health had made great strides since then, new social problems had certainly arisen; and even the health experts seemed powerless to deal with creeping blight and air pollution. Housing code enforcement had made headway, but without adequate rehousing facilities this had often meant less reasonably-priced accommodation rather than more. Metropolitan coordination of objectives simply did not exist; as Paul Ylvisaker, erstwhile head of the social-policy division of the Ford Foundation put it, improvements in city life should have been tackled on an areawide basis, and, to be effective, combined with minute attention to the smallest neighborhood groupings at the same time. It was becoming clear that America's unwillingness to deal with the city as a whole (as it had done in its multifunctional attack on problems of the TVA) were due partly to lingering racial antagonisms, partly to the anti-city attitudes of suburban homeowners, and partly to the pursuit of middle-class interests by city governments, to the evident exclusion of the interests of the urban poor.

Under such circumstances, it is no wonder that the future city could be envisaged as a series of segregated "projects" or single-function areas, surrounded by a mosaic of separated subdivisions extending outward into the urban-rural fringe, served only by personalized transportation, i.e., the self-driven, privately owned automobile. All predictions pointed to the fact that when the Interstate Highway System reached completion in 1972, sums equalling or surpassing its $47,000,000,000 cost would be appropriated for a new program, this time concentrating more heavily on the improvement of city arterials and other types of road within the great urban belts of the United States. This would bring more traffic in and through the central cities, carving them up still further; in fact, it was becoming increasingly difficult to estimate what percentage of residential use could remain there with the increasing demand for urban land by other types of development.

An overview of comparable trends in American urbanization has created an attitude among social scientists leading to the surmise that the classical image of the city is now no longer useful. Kenneth Boulding, professor of economics at the University of Michigan, is a spokesman for this attitude. The need for concentration has disappeared, he says, and, in fact, concentration is asking for destruction in the age of the H-bomb. The main need for continuing concentration, face-to-face communication, will disappear as soon as messages carried by modulated light beams become practicable. Boulding visualizes a society in which population is spread evenly over the globe in almost self-sufficient households, each with immediate communication channels to libraries, cultural facilities, and any individual on the face of the earth. Admitting that such ideas may be pure science fiction,

Boulding nevertheless suggests that if they came about, men would probably want to recreate the classical city purely for purposes of pleasure; and he sees this tendency in embryo in the movement of the rich back into the old centers and the development of the shopping mall.[3]

Indeed, it is difficult to imagine a world without centers or central places, and Professor Boulding's retrieval libraries would probably be located in association with other useful facilities. It is not a happy picture, as he admits in his subtitle: "A Frightened Look at Post-Civilization." In the showing of what technology can produce in terms of the future, a vastly important ingredient of the social system can be overlooked: its political aspect. It is all very exciting to think that by 1980 personal transportation can be accomplished on Ground Effect Machines, or that by the year 2000, when our population will have doubled, we shall be colonizing the planets. (When has colonization *not* been turned to in times of overpopulation?) Even the idea of cyborgs (described by Arthur C. Clark in his book *Profiles of the Future*), half-man, half-machine, does not seem too strange in an age of artificial hearts and iron lungs. But the centralized political control that would be needed to complete Professor Boulding's picture is not so palatable. It is impossible to imagine a society like Martin Buber's, composed of social units of urban and rural workers living and producing on a communal basis, being able to exist in Boulding's spread-out, isolated urban dot map. Yet a naive faith in technology must nowadays be added to the beliefs, myths, and social attitudes recorded in Chapter 1.

The difference between absolute order and collective order is well-expressed in the conflicts that are shaping today's cities. And it may be said at once that predictions—such as that by the year 2000 the United States will be 90 percent urban, or that half the world will have starved to death—although they may be intensely sobering, have only indirect bearing on what course the cities will take. Much more important are the goals which an urbanized society must adopt in shaping its environment. If there is no possibility of agreement, then a kind of entropy or dissolving of the city's structure may set in; but if Americans can

[3] Kenneth E. Boulding, "The Death of the City," in *The Historian and the City*. (Oscar Handlin and John Burchard, eds.) (Cambridge, Mass., 1963).

decide that they want cities the lateral expansion of which shall be held within certain limits, or that a balance between the natural and the urban environment shall be maintained, or that the centers shall be beautiful as well as healthy—they will spend the money and do the work to attain these goals. Society's aims will have to change; and its attitude to land-holding, to urban collective bargaining, and to urban government (which will discharge the functions of adjustment and administration only while citizen groups perform the constructive tasks) will be critical for the future development of cities. Their forms will reflect these goals, just as the form of the modern American city at its inception reflected the goals of the post-Civil War business and architectural world.

Meanwhile, until the voice of the city dweller can be heard in a collective sense, it is best to cry "Halt!" to schemes which further disrupt its patterns. In certain periods the best action is to sit down firmly in the road of "progress," blocking its agents in their task. This is what Mayor Richard C. Lee, in a literal rather than a figurative manner, urged the Negro population of New Haven to do in the streets which commuters to the central city used on their way home to the suburbs, to dramatize the city's plight. (*See Readings Nos. 41 and 42.*)

The Role of the City. Looking back at what has been called the Age of Optimism, the Good Years, the Gilded Age, and other sobriquets of a cheerful nature, it is easy to fall into the manner of regarding our own as the Age of Anxiety, especially in the troubled cities. There are great contrasts, to be sure. When the modern American city emerged in the long period of reconstruction after the Civil War, the nation itself was being forged into a world economic power. Between 1860 and 1953 net income from manufacturing rose 4,500 percent. The cities themselves, suffering as they frequently did from the effects of recurring depressions, were looked upon as centers of commerce and industry. The locus of activity has now shifted; and although the central city remains important in a financial sense, it has lost part of the mystique associated with the seat of power. Add to this the concentration of deprived people within its borders:

"where childhood dreams of joy lie dead"

and you have the present-day city of anomie, of black ghettoes, or of violence and mob rule.

And yet . . . there remains the vision of the City on a Hill. There is a will to make the city a better place. Instead of fleeing the cities, as a group of Christian Socialists fled San Francisco to found the Utopian colony of Altruria in 1894, church ministers in many cities are in the forefront of urban housing and other central-city activities, continuing a tradition which dates back to the waves of immigration in the 1880's and 1890's. There are Jewish community centers and Quaker half-way houses for released offenders and a whole new profession of community organizers, whose duties involve making city life possible for newly arrived Puerto Ricans or for those who will never find the pot of gold at the end of the rainbow.

For the city continues to be a magnet, a center of the aspirations of man. If this chronicle had only one message, it would be that the city since the Civil War must be thought of as our most important *cultural* phenomenon, and, as such, treated with respect for its history and traditions. We have learned that even the slum is a fragile and carefully wrought network of human interrelationships—which the bulldozer can destroy in one afternoon; that the Negro ghetto has a system of values that will not be present when its residents are forced into other parts of town. We know that the city *can* be beautiful because men in cities have always tried to create beauty, and that this beauty is reflected in those buildings and parks which can truly be said to be works of art.

We know too that society must have standards, and that these standards must equal those of the men who first forged a nation out of many colonies and who envisaged a capital city worthy of the national aim. This aim encompassed the needs of many and diverse groups and peoples, and was antithetical to cities, homes, and persons being cast into one mold or way of life. "In my father's house are many mansions," and there should be a place for everyone inside. Those who do not recognize or choose to ignore these cultural requirements—the wreckers of the city, the new barbarians—should never be allowed to touch the precious fabric. A new generation of city planners will be sensitive to these values. The new planners will remember the importance of Charles E. Merriam's admonition: "In a national state, and especially in a democracy, it is of the highest importance that the necessary role of local self-government in matters that are really local should be protected and preserved"—realizing that this has come to mean neighborhood participation in decisions affecting housing, mental health, or highway routes, as well as actual engagement in the process of urban renewal. At the same time, the planners will heed McIver's observation that the definition of community must involve the whole area in which men live their lives, go to work, or play; and that this area has expanded to take in the entire urban region. There must therefore be plans at the scale of the region (long overdue), design at a regional scale, regional economic development, regional health plans (underway), regional theaters, regional recreation parks, seacoast regions, river-valley regions, and other regional activities transcending local boundaries.

At the same time there will be minute questions of residential infill, small-scale residential surgery, and public debate on the merits of new building in relation to the existing residential pattern. This will take place on a neighborhood scale, with full neighborhood participation. Planners, architects, engineers, technicians, mayors, local bosses, do-gooders, and merchants, state legislators and members of Congress—all will have to learn a new way of community planning; and it is not the easy way of unfulfilled promise, or, alternatively, of cut-and-slash.

Until the mayors listen to their ignored constituency, until the middle-income groups learn to consider their neighbors over the hill instead of pretending that the poor don't exist, until architects give up building exclusively for boards of directors and for the nonobjective client, until local operators stop destroying historic buildings, and until the engineers are made to listen to the poets, we may expect the city to face even worse prospects than at present. Meanwhile . . . .

The continuing American city remains a stronghold of the collective spirit—diverse, disputative, and loyal to group and civic values. It has always been venal, but the tinsel values of the marketplace rate lower there than the hucksters would have us believe. Something of the spirit of a very large family still exists —a family of rich and varied traditions, in which the pioneers are as respected as the builders of what we see today. There are lessons to be learned from the early citizens: a landscape architect calling for pure air in the industrial city, a rich man donating his collection of old masters to the public, an architect building a magnificent gateway to the city in the form of a classical railroad terminus. Many and fabulous are the things to be admired, wondrous are the acts of humanity and sacrifice to be cherished. The modern American city has been since its inception the locus of American hope for the future. It remains so; and its replacement has not yet been found.

Part II
READINGS

The Urban Agglomeration[1]

Local government has been described as the maverick of American politics. Its arbitrary ways are reflected in the great numbers of special districts and overlapping jurisdictions— federal, state, local, and private. In attempting to analyze a particular city, therefore, one must also be familiar with its more important socio-economic institutions, and, in examining these, know which are dominating or in control in any given period or situation. In Boston, the leadership of State Street could be counted on for almost a hundred years; this is no longer true. In the following example, the influx of a residential population has wrenched the earlier Virginia town life out of context and thrown local domination of the political scene into new hands. The land has become part of Metropolitan Washington, a fact of political life both resisted and acclaimed, depending on the special interest of local factions whose makeup turns largely on the ways people make their living, travel to work, and educate their children.

In America the incorporated municipalities of a century ago were substantially identical with urban areas. The identification and demarcation of cities and towns thus offered no difficulties to census takers, statisticians, or city dwellers themselves. By contrast, to illustrate present needs for new criteria of classification, let us compare Falls Church, Virginia, with the "largest city in the world."

Falls Church is known to many residents of nearby Washington, D.C., as a vaguely defined section that interposes a traffic bottleneck on the way to the Virginia Skyline Drive. The incorporated city of about 2 square miles and some 10,000 inhabitants is rarely distinguished from East Falls Church, a section of Arlington County; from West Falls Church, within its own boundaries; from the Falls Church District of Fairfax County,

[1] Stuart A. Rice, "Problems in the Statistics of Urban Agglomeration," *Science*, 128 (Nov. 7, 1958), pp. 1-2.

with some 20,000 or 30,000 population; or from the area served
by the Falls Church post office, an area containing, perhaps
60,000 people, all of whom use Falls Church as their postal address. To add further confusion, the city's own high school is
outside its boundaries, in Fairfax County, a wholly separate
jurisdiction in the Virginia setting, while "Falls Church High
School," located within the city, is a property of Fairfax County
and subject to that county's jurisdiction.

If the identity of Falls Church is obscure, even to many residents, the "largest city in the world" is virtually unknown in this
country. In area it is 12 times as large as Falls Church, but has
only about three times the population of Falls Church. This
"city" is Kiruna, Sweden. It includes within its municipal boundaries iron mines, the highest mountain in Sweden, and much of
the northern territory of that country. By legal definition Falls
Church and Kiruna are both "cities," with taxing and administrative authorities. In other respects they have little comparability.
If attention is shifted from public administration to the demographic, social, and economic realities with which urban life is
increasingly concerned, it seems clear that legal status as a mu-
nicipality is no longer adequate as a statistical criterion for the
classification of spatial groupings of people. New criteria are
developing new conceptual units, and the end is not yet
visible. . . .

It was in the census of 1900 that the Bureau of the Census,
with remarkable prescience in its adaptation to change, for the
first time defined a new demographic unit, the "metropolitan
district." As cities increasingly emptied or attracted inhabitants
into surrounding areas, the use of this new concept as a statistical
unit for all manner of social and economic analyses gained momentum. It is not improbable that "standard metropolitan areas,"
successors to "metropolitan districts," now outrank "cities" in
statistical importance. . . .[1a]

[1a] In the Census of 1960 the term is Standard Metropolitan Statistical
    Area.

Founding of the Capital
and Speculation in the 1830's

The Republic came into being with an enthusiasm which was reflected in its zest for building and planning. Washington's hope for the new capital city on the Potomac was that it would emerge as a world port, serving all the hinterland as far as the Great Lakes, to which it would be connected by a system of canals. Jefferson's wish was that it might surpass in beauty all earlier capitals, and that, like Babylon, it should be built "four-square." He had introduced the grid system to the rest of the country in the Land Ordinance of 1785.

The early history of the capital was not without speculation for gain, which was considered the best way of obtaining rapid urban growth; but the auctions and lot sales languished, and Washington lacked the urbanity of a true capital for almost a hundred years. The importance of the city as a symbol, however, enshrined the virtues of real estate speculation in the public mind, so much so that to this day municipalities in the United States seldom hold any land for future development, unlike many of the cities of northwestern Europe. James Silk Buckingham's description of land-jobbing on the other side of the Potomac, although perhaps apocryphal, is nevertheless typical of thousands of land booms engineered in unpromising locations throughout the nineteenth century.

By THOMAS JEFFERSON [2]

. . . a territory not exceeding 10. miles square (or, I presume, 100 square miles in any form) to be located by metes and bounds.

3. commissioners to be appointed
I suppose them not entitled to any salary.

   [if they live near the place they may, in some instances, be influenced by self interest, & partialities: but they will push the work with zeal. if they are from a distance, & northwardly, they will be more impartial, but may affect delays.]
the Commissioners to purchase or accept 'such quantity of land on the E. side of the river as the President shall deem *proper for the U.S.*' viz. for the federal Capitol, the offices, the President's house & gardens, the town house, Market house, publick walks, hospital. for the Presidents's house, offices & gardens, I should think 2. squares sould be consolidated. for the Capitol & offices one square. for the Market one square. for the Public walks 9. squares consolidated.

   the expression 'such quantity of land as the President shall deem *proper for the U.S.*' is vague. it may therefore be extended to the acceptance or purchase of land enough for the town: and I have no doubt it is the wish, & perhaps expectation. in that case it will be to be laid out in lots & streets. I should propose these to be at right angles as in Philadelphia, & that no street be narrower than 100. feet, with foot-ways of 15. feet. where a street is long & level, it might be 120. feet wide. I should prefer squares of at least 200. yards every way, which will be of about 8. acres each.

   The Commissioners should have some taste in architecture, because they may have to decide between different plans. . . .

   In locating the town, will it not be best to give it double the extent on the eastern branch of what it has on the river? the former will be for persons in commerce, the latter for those connected with the Government.

[2] Note of Thomas Jefferson: "Proceedings to be had under the Residence Act," November 29, 1790, in *Records* (U.S. v. Morris), Vol. VII, pp. 2155-9, as quoted by Saul K. Padover in *Thomas Jefferson and the National Capital* (Washington: United States Government Printing Office, 1946), pp. 30-31, 35-36.

Will it not be best to lay out the long streets parallel with the creek, and the other crossing them at right angles, so as to leave no oblique angled lots but the single row which shall be on the river? thus:

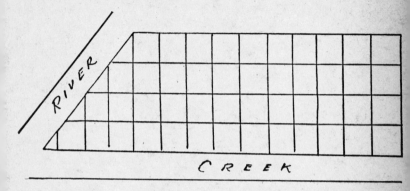

By JAMES SILK BUCKINGHAM [3]

An idea was conceived by some real admirer or sycophantic flatterer of General Jackson . . . , that it would be well to set up a rival city on the south of the Potomac, to eclipse Washington on the north, and to call it by the name of the rival chief. This idea was at once acted on by the immediate survey of the spot, where the bridge touches the shore, and being a perfect level, a city was soon mapped and planned on paper, with squares, avenues, markets, an exchange, churches, and all the usual accompaniments of a large emporium; General Jackson was applied to, for his patronage to the undertaking, which was readily granted; and, thus provided, the individual, who got up the whole, sent on to New York, where the rage for speculating in lands and city-lots was at its highest; and forthwith a number of those gentlemen came here, to purchase. When they had bought their lots, at high prices, they repaired back to New York, to sell them to other speculators at still higher; and General Jackson having, at the request of the founder, attended the ceremony of laying the foundation of the Exchange of Jackson

[3] James Silk Buckingham, *America, Historical, Statistic and Descriptive,* Vol. 1 (London, 1841), pp. 372-374.

City, before a single dwelling of any kind was erected, and delivered a long oration on the occasion, the lots rose in value, because the city had been actually begun; and buyer after buyer continued to give a higher and higher price. At length, however, the sums per foot given for this waste land were so extravagant, that no further advances could be had upon it, and the last buyer consequently found himself stuck fast, and could only get out of his difficulty at an immense sacrifice. . . . [A comment of last auctioneer on marsh that existed there] . . . so rich that it produced sixty bushels of frogs to the acre . . . there was no need of incurring expense for fencing, as there were alligators enough on the spot to form an excellent fence, *if you* could catch them, by planting them with their heads downward and their tails in the air.

READINGS NOS. 4 AND 5

Transportation in the 1840's

Although by the mid-nineteenth century the urbanization of the United States was well on its way, the ante-bellum period is often looked back on as a golden age. The coming of the industrial revolution and the first railroads were nevertheless beginning to disrupt and transform the cities of the early Republic with their solid brick rows and streets of white clapboard houses. Edgar Allan Poe records the coming of brownstone to New York as "a desecration" brought on by "the spirit of Improvement"; and both he and Mrs. Stowe observe changes in transportation as a mixed blessing, just as at the end of the century the novelist William Dean Howells was to fulminate against the uproar of the horse-drawn omnibuses and express wagons underneath the rattling steam locomotives of the New York "El."

By HARRIET BEECHER STOWE [4]

Such confusion of tongues, such shouting and swearing, such want of all sort of system and decency in arrangements, I never

[4] Harriet Beecher Stowe, *Life of Harriet Beecher Stowe* (Boston, 1891), p. 107.

desire to see again. I was literally almost trodden down and torn to pieces in the Rochester depot when I went to help my poor, near-sighted spouse in sorting out the baggage. You see there was an accident which happened to the cars leaving Rochester that morning, which kept us two hours and a half at the passing place this side of Auburn, waiting for them to come up and go by us. The consequence was that we got into this Rochester depot aforesaid after dark, and the steam-boat, the canal-boat, and the Western train of cars had all been kept waiting three hours beyond their usual time, and they all broke loose upon us the moment we put our heads out of the cars, and such a jerking, and elbowing, and scuffling, and swearing, and protesting, and scolding you never heard, while the great locomotive sailed up and down in the midst thereof, spitting fire and smoke like some great fiend monster diverting himself with our commotions. . . .

By EDGAR ALLAN POE [5]

The din of the vehicles, however, is even more thoroughly, and more intolerably a nuisance. Are we never to have done with these unmeaning round stones?—than which a more ingenious contrivance for driving men mad through sheer noise, was undoubtedly never invented. It is difficult to foresee what mode of street-pavement will come, finally, into vogue; but we should have *some* change, and that forthwith, or we must have new and more plentiful remedies for headache. The twelve-inch cubes of stone (square, with the upper surface roughened) make, perhaps, the most durable, and in many respects, the best road; they are, however, expensive, and the noise they emit is objectionable, although in a much less degree than the round stones. Of the stereatomic wooden pavement, we hear nothing, now, at all. The people seem to have given it up altogether—but nothing better could be invented. We inserted the blocks, without preparation, and they failed. Therefore, we abandoned the experiment. Had they been Kyanized [treated with corrosive sublimate] the result would have been very different, and the wooden causeways would have been in extensive use throughout the country.

[5] Edgar Allan Poe, *Doings of Gotham,* collected by Jacob E. Spannuth (Pottsville, Pennsylvania, 1929), pp. 61-62.

The Picturesque City: 1864 and 1884

The American idea of progress in urban life has strong links with social darwinism. The course is upward, from a primitive past. After the Civil War, the doctrines of Herbert Spencer, who taught the survival of the fittest in business life, took firm hold. The change in emphasis from cultural to material progress can be discerned in the two following excerpts, taken twenty years apart, although a distinction should be made between the charming pleasures of Detroit life in the mid-eighties and the grosser commercialism of today. It may also be noted that the remnants of Judge Woodward's plan, modeled on that of Washington, D.C., and as a total concept defeated by Detroit speculators, remained through the nineteenth century as a setting for fashion and the beau monde.

By HENRY T. TUCKERMAN [6]

What a contrast! This meeting of the New York Historical Society and that which was held some fifty years ago. Ponder awhile upon the circumstances which mark this difference. At the period at which our first organization took place, this city contained about sixty thousand inhabitants; at present it embraces some seven hundred and fifty thousand inhabitants. A large majority of the residents dwelt below Cortlandt Street and Maiden Lane. A sparse population then occupied that portion of the island which lies above the site of the New York Hospital on Broadway; and the grounds now covered with the magnificent edifices which ornament Upper Broadway, the Fifth Avenue, Fourteenth Street, Union Place, and Madison Square, were graced with the sycamore, the elm, the oak, the chestnut, the wild cherry, the peach, the pear, and the plum tree, and further ornamented with gardens appropriated to horticultural products, with here and there the artichoke, the tulip, and the sun-flower.

[6] Henry T. Tuckerman, *Old New York: or, Reminiscences of the Past Sixty Years* (New York, 1865).

Where now stand our Astor Library, the Mercantile Library, the New York Medical College, the Academy of Music, the Medical University of the State, Cooper's Institute, and the Bible Society House, the old gardens of our Dutch ancestors were most abundant, cultivated with something of the artistic regularity of the Hollanders, luxuriating in the sweet marjoram, the mint, the thyme, the currant, and the gooseberry. The banks of our majestic rivers on either side presented deep and abrupt declivities, and the waters adjacent were devoted to the safety of the floating timber, brought down from the Mohawk, on the Hudson River, or elsewhere obtained, on the Connecticut, in mighty rafts, designed for naval architecture and house-building. Our avenues, squares, and leading roads, were not yet laid out by Morris, Clinton, and Rutherford, and our street regulations in paving and sidewalks, even in those passes or highways now most populous, had reached but little above the Park, and in the Bowery only within the precincts of Baynard street. The present City Hall was in a state of erection, and so circumscribed, at that time, was the idea of the City's progress, that the Common Council, by a slender majority, decided that the postern part of the Hall should be composed of red stone, inasmuch as it was not likely to attract much notice from the scattered inhabitants who might reside above Chambers Street. . . .

New York in the past affords us innumerable precious memories and honorable achievements; New York in the future may, through the loyalty of her faithful children, reach a height of auspicious renown, commensurate with her mercantile fame, her historical significance, and her material prosperity. The Dutch gable ends have disappeared, the unpretending hospitality has vanished, the rural vicinage is demolished; Peter Stuyvesant's pear tree is the last relic of suburban gardens; theology has ramified, and in so doing mitigated its rancor; physic has multiplied her disciples; law has acquired a thousand clever, for a dozen brilliant votaries; the opera has outvied the drama; rents have become fabulous; land has risen in value beyond all precedent; Yankees have driven out burgomasters; Cuban segars Holland pipes; railways old fashioned gigs, and omnibuses family chariots: the tonsorial occupation is all but superseded by the perpetual holiday of beards; and skirts, instead of being gathered up as of old, sway in fixed expansion on the encroaching hoop;

turbans, shoe-buckles, cures, the pillory, spinning-wheels, and short ruffles are obsolete, while the "last of the cocked hats" is visible in our streets; but the good old Knickerbocker honesty and geniality may yet be found by some firesides. We have eloquent proof that Washington's memory is still tenderly revered, that Franklin's maxims are yet reliable, that Hamilton's political sagacity and chivalry are not forgotten, that Fulton's inventive genius and DeWitt Clinton's comprehensive polity are still appreciated; and while this remains true, New York "still lives," the New York where the principle of internal improvement was initiated, the liberty of the press earliest recognized, and the first President of the republic inaugurated. . . .

By ROBERT E. ROBERTS [7]

The city outside the business centre, from this point, has the appearance of a dense forest with many heaven-pointing spires towering above the trees, justifying what has been said that Detroit is a park city, for were the buildings removed it would be an extensive park, with more than two hundred miles of driveways, forming a perfect network. . . . That dense cluster of trees about 1,000 feet distant to the northwest are in the two Grand Circus Parks, with a large fountain in the centre of each, where on any day or evening during the heated term, may be seen the numerous settees filled with citizens, the gravel walks with promenaders and numbers of maidens with perambulators giving infants the benefit of breathing in the open air, sheltered from the hot rays of the sun, pure and wholesome atmosphere. Bands discourse cheering music occasionally from the grand stand there provided, and the electric lights give brilliancy to the scene. Radiating from these parks are six avenues, one of 120 feet and three 200 feet in width, each skirted with rows of stately trees, and Woodward avenue, 120 feet, passes between, dividing the parks. . . .

Within the past three score years there have come to us the following useful devices and discoveries: The steel carriage spring, in place of the leather thorough-braces and spring pole; the locomotive and palace car, in place of the corduroy and McAdam road; the electric telegraph; the steam reaper and

[7] Robert E. Roberts, *City of the Straits* (Detroit, 1884), pp. 120-122, 148-149.

thrasher, in place of the cradle and flail; the percussion cap and breech-loader, in place of the flint-lock musket; the petroleum and electric light, in place of the tallow dip and whale oil rush-light; the "loco-foco" or friction lighter in place of flint, steel and tinder box; palace steam ferries, in place of the horse-boat and canoe plying across our majestic river. And in this ancient city of the strait we have the coach, 'bus, coupe, and buggy, in place

> "Of French charettes bouncing along, *les filles*
> All seated *à la Turque* upon the soft
> Warm buffaloes, and bobbing up and down
> With each jerk of that relic of the Old Regime."

READING NO. 8

Architectural "Rationalism" in the United States[8]

Henry Van Brunt (1832-1903) was a student in R. M. Hunt's office before the Civil War. His best known architectural work is Memorial Hall at Harvard University. As translator of Viollet-le-Duc's Discourses, *Van Brunt introduced the French restorer's theory of rationalism or honesty of construction to the United States, with emphasis on the Gothic and the picturesque. Later, Van Brunt's own architecture went through a Romanesque phase and then a classic manner. His firm designed the Electricity Building at the Chicago World's Fair of 1893.*

The master-workman, however, laid aside his functions as an originator, and the architect was born, when precedent began so to accumulate, when civilization became so complex and exacting, the wants of mankind so various and conflicting, that, to

---

[8] Eugene Emmanuel Viollet-le-Duc, *Discourses on Architecture,* translated, with an introductory essay by Henry Van Brunt (Boston: James R. Osgood and Company, 1875), pp. xii-xiii.

meet the more elaborate emergencies of building, there came to
be needed a larger and more exact knowledge, a more careful
study of plans and details, and a more deliberate and scientific
method of construction. These conditions began to render essential the organization of some processes and appliances, by means
of which the system of structure in each case, embracing all the
details of the building, could be more exactly and completely set
forth long before the first stone was laid. They implied, in short,
draughtsmen, instruments of mathematical precision, a library
of reference, and all the other appointments and conveniences
of an office, that is, both of a studio and of a place of business.
They implied, moreover, not only the unwritten experience of
the builder, but the training and observation of the scholar, by
means of which the most remote results could be foreseen and
provided for; and more especially, they called for the feeling,
the inspiration, the patience, self-denial, and tempered zeal of
the artist. Uncultured genius may be eloquent, but its eloquence
is ungrammatical; and although in architecture as in literature
we may sometimes pardon the awkwardness of the phrase for
the sake of the preciousness of the thought, in neither—and more
especially in architecture, whose highest duty it is to embody history and civilization in durable monuments, and whose processes
are so artificial and scientific—can the preciousness of the thought
render less necessary purity of language, elegance of expression,
and exactness of knowledge. Uncultured genius may in a moment
of heaven-sent inspiration invent a great architectural thought,
but plodding culture is needed to give it such expression as to
render it worthy of place in the records of time and capable of
doing duty as a new starting-point of architectural style. This
is the plain raison d'etre of the architect. He exists because
civilization demands him. It is our present duty to see that he
is worthy of his mission. . . .

Hunt the Innovator I[9]

Richard Morris Hunt (1828-1895), the brother of the painter William Morris Hunt, was the most influential architect of the first phase of the classic revival. He was known best as architect to the Vanderbilt family, and his first great house inspired by the early French Renaissance chateaux was built on Fifth Avenue, New York (1879-1881). Marble House and The Breakers at Newport, Rhode Island, as well as his masterpiece, Biltmore near Ashville, North Carolina, are others of his Vanderbilt commissions. The foundations of Biltmore spread over five acres of ground and are surrounded by landscaped groves designed by Olmsted. It was the last commission for both men.

Hunt's public work includes the Metropolitan Museum of Art and the Administration Building at the World's Fair of 1893. (See Reading No. 19.)

Hunt, who found his taste for Classic work opposed by the wave of Gothic and 'Picturesque' popularity, had meantime compromised with the public by taking into association with himself Henry O. Avery, and together they produced the designs for the William K. Vanderbilt house, Marquand house, and others in the French transitional styles of Francis I and Louis XII. The Vanderbilt house was very successful, one of the most charming designs I have seen, either old or modern, in the style. Henry P. Kirby, of New York, produced some fine imaginative studies in this style, which he published in his book of 'Compositions'. A number of strong men were won over to the style of the Early French Renaissance, including Ellis (Harvey Ellis), who produced some interesting work in St. Louis, among other things the City Hall; Bruce Price, of New York, who designed the Château Frontenac, an hotel for the Canadian Pacific Railway at Quebec; and Clarence Luce of New York, Louis Hickman of Philadelphia, Julius Schweinfurth and George Newton of Boston,

[9] Francis S. Swales, "American Architecture: with Especial Reference to Work at Washington," *Journal of the RIBA,* series 3, 16 (1909), pp. 334-335.

made studies of conspicuous merit, nearly all of which were produced between the years 1888 and 1892. . . . The atelier system, first attempted by Richard Hunt, was successfully inaugurated about fifteen years ago (by Mr. E. L. Masqueray, Chief Architect of the St. Louis Exposition, 1903, who was at the time Hunt's chief assistant), and has been fostered by the Society of Beaux-Arts Architects, which has made its principal objective the education of the younger men. . . .

READINGS NOS. 10, 11, AND 12

The Municipal Park Movement, 1850-1900

Although Andrew Jackson Downing, the celebrated landscape gardener of the Romantic age, died in 1852 and did not live to see the reality, he was an early advocate of a central park for New York. The flavor of his voluminous writings is contained in this excerpt of 1856.

Frederick Law Olmsted (1822-1903) and Calvert Vaux, Downing's English partner, won the competition for their design of Central Park in 1858, thereafter going on to design parks and parkways in cities all over North America. Olmsted's favorite was Prospect Park in Brooklyn, begun in 1866; the excerpt given below from the landscape architects' report reveals the socio-psychological interest which distinguishes Olmsted from run-of-the-mill professionals of his period.

By the end of the century the park "system" had been devised. This American invention owes much to Olmsted's genius; nevertheless, a comprehensive system of open spaces connected with encircling parkways and boulevards derives also from Second Empire Paris, a city which had renewed itself between 1850 and 1870. Governor John Evans of Denver records both the novelty and the challenge with which public acquisition of land for non-business purposes confronted western American cities.

John Evans (1814-1897) represents as well as any individual the spirit of civic enterprise which counterpoises the graft and corruption of the post-Civil War period. As a medical student in

*the Midwest, he began to revolutionize professional practice, be-
ing credited with inventing an Obstetrical Extractor, and he helped
to reveal cholera as a communicable disease. The city of Evanston, Illinois, is named after him. As governor of the Territory,
he made Denver a great railroad center, and as a city-builder he
made it the permanent capital of Colorado. As a regional planner
he induced the federal government to deepen the channel into
Galveston, Texas, and by extending his Denver and New Orleans
Railroad to Galveston, he made Denver a port of entry for international trade. He was an abolitionist, a crusader for women's
rights, and a university founder.*

By ANDREW JACKSON DOWNING [10]

We have said nothing of the social influence of such a great
park in New York. But this is really the most interesting phase
of the whole matter. It is a fact, not a little remarkable, that,
ultra democratic as are the political tendencies of America, its
most intelligent social tendencies are almost wholly in a contrary
direction. And among the topics discussed by the advocates and
opponents of the new park, none seem so poorly understood as
the social aspect of the thing. It is indeed both curious and amus-
ing to see the stand taken on the one hand by the million, that
the park is made for the "upper ten," who ride in the fine car-
riages; and, on the other hand, by the wealthy and refined, that
a park in this country, will be "usurped by rowdies and low
people." Shame upon our republican compatriots, who so little
understand the elevating influences of the beautiful in nature and
in art, when enjoyed in common by thousands and hundreds of
thousands of all classes without distinction! They can never have
seen, how, all over France and Germany the whole population
of the cities pass their afternoons and evenings together, in the
beautiful parks and gardens. How they enjoy together the same
music, breathe the same atmosphere of art, enjoy the same scenery, and grow into social freedom by the very influences of easy
intercourse, space and beauty that surround them. In Germany,
especially, they have never seen how the highest and lowest par-

[10] Egbert L. Viele (Engineer-in-Chief), to the Commissioners of the
Central Park (Fernando Wood, Mayor; Joseph S. Taylor, Street
Commissioner), *Board of Aldermen, Document No. 5* (New York,
January 19, 1857), pp. 162-164.

take alike of the common enjoyment—the prince seated beneath the trees on a rush-bottomed chair, before a little wooden table, supping his coffee or his ice, with the same freedom from state and pretension as the simplest subject. Drawing-room conventionalities are too narrow for a mile or two of spacious garden landscape, and one can be happy with ten thousand in the social freedom of a community of genial influences, without the unutterable pang of not having been introduced to the company present.

These social doubters, who thus intrench themselves in the sole citadel of exclusiveness in republican America, mistake our people and their destiny. If we would but have listened to them, our magnificent river and lake steamers, those real places of the million, would have no velvet couches, no splendid mirrors, no luxurious carpets. Such costly and rare appliances of civilization, they would have told us, could only be rightly used by the privileged families of wealth, and would be trampled upon and utterly ruined by the democracy of the country, who travel one hundred miles for half a dollar. And yet these, our floating palaces and our monster hotels, with their purple and fine linen, are they not respected by the majority who use them, as truly as other palaces by their rightful sovereigns? Alas! for the faithlessness of the few, who possess, regarding the capacity for culture of the many, who are wanting. Even upon the lower platform of liberty and education, that the masses stand in Europe, we see the elevating influences of a wide popular enjoyment; of galleries of art; public libraries, parks and gardens, which have raised the people in social civilization and social culture to a far higher level than we have yet attained in republican America. And yet, this broad ground of popular refinement must be taken in republican America, for it belongs of right more truly here than elsewhere. It is republican in its very idea and tendency. It takes up popular education where the common school and ballot-box leave it, and raises up the working-man to the same level of enjoyment with the man of leisure and accomplishment. The higher social and artistic elements of every man's nature lie dormant within him, and every laborer is a possible gentleman, not by the possession of money or fine clothes—but through the refining influence of intellectual and moral culture. Open wide therefore, the doors of your libraries and picture galleries, all ye true republicans! Build halls where knowledge shall be freely diffused among men, and not shut up within the narrow walls of narrower institutions. Plant spacious parks in your cities, and unloose their gates as wide as the gates of morning to the whole people. As there are no dark places at noon day, so education and culture—the true sunshine of the soul—will banish the plague spots of democracy; and the dread of the ignorant exclusive who has no faith in the refinement of a republic, will stand abashed in the next century, before a whole people whose system of voluntary education embraces (combined with perfect individual freedom) not only common schools of rudimentary knowledge, but common enjoyments of all classes in the higher realms of art, letters, science, social recreations and enjoyments. Were our legislatures but wise enough to understand today, the destinies of the New World, the gentility of Sir Philip Sidney, made universal, would be not half so much a miracle fifty years hence in America, as the idea of a whole nation of laboring men reading and writing, was, in his day, in England.

By FREDERICK LAW OLMSTED [11]

In the present century, not only have the old parks been thus maintained, but many new parks have been formed with these purposes exclusively in view, especially within and adjoining considerable towns, and it is upon our knowledge of these latter that our simplest conception of a town park is founded. It is from experience in these that all our ideas of parks must spring.

This experience shows that the great advantage which a town finds in a park, lies in the addition to the health, strength and morality which comes from it to its people, an advantage which is not only in itself very great and positive but which as certainly results in an increase of material wealth as good harvests or active commerce. And the reason is obvious: all wealth is the result of labor, and every man's individual wealth is, on the whole, increased by the labor of every other in the community, supposing it to be wisely and honestly applied; but as there cannot be the slightest use of the will, of choice between two actions or two words, nor the slightest exercise of skill of any kind, without the expenditure of force, it follows that, without recu-

[11] Olmsted, Vaux and Co., *Report of the Landscape Architects* (Brooklyn, New York, 1866), pp. 15-16.

peration and recreation of force, the power of each individual to labor wisely and honestly is soon lost, and that, without the recuperation of force, the power of each individual to add to the wealth of the community is, as a necessary consequence, also soon lost.

But to this process of recuperation a condition is necessary known since the days of Aesop, as the unbending of the faculties which have been tasked, and this *unbending* of the faculties we find is impossible, except by the occupation of the imagination with objects and reflections of a quite different character from those which are associated with their bent condition. To secure such a diversion of the imagination, the best possible stimulus is found to be the presentation of a class of objects to the perceptive organs, which shall be as agreeable as possible to the taste, and at the same time entirely different from the objects connected with those occupations by which the faculties have been tasked. And this is what is found by townspeople in a park.

If now we ask further, what the qualities of a park are which fit it to meet this requirement? we find two circumstances, common to all parks, in distinction from other places in towns, namely, scenery offering the most agreeable contrast to that of the rest of the town, and opportunity for people to come together for the single purpose of enjoyment, unembarrassed by the limitations with which they are surrounded at home, or in the pursuit of their daily avocations, or of such amusements as are elsewhere offered.

By JOHN EVANS [12]

History is repeating itself in the lifetime of one individual. I was active in starting many of the important enterprises of Chicago for nearly twenty years. President Lincoln then, by appointing me Governor, sent me thirty-two years ago to Pikes Peak, the Territory of Colorado. I found Denver a shanty town of twelve or fifteen hundred inhabitants. I have since then labored faithfully to build up the city, and develop the wonderful resources of the state. Their development, and the growth of the

[12] Walter Dill Scott, *John Evans: an appreciation,* quoted by Edgar Carlisle McMechan in *The Life of John Evans* (Evanston, Illinois, privately printed by courtesy of Lester J. Norris, 1939), pp. 33-34.

city, are only partially begun, and we have come to the period of preparing a system of parks. The first step in the operation must be the purchase of land, sufficient for a grand system. It will take long years to improve the parks. Afterward the parks cannot be had without the land, and the longer the purchase is delayed the more the land will cost; and if Denver grows rapidly, as it is sure to do, the land will grow in price in a geometrical ratio, so that the interest on the price will be a mere bagatelle compared with the increase in value of the land. The discussion in the papers, and individual opinions given in the last few days, have carried me back to the more bitter discussion of the question in Chicago—and the similarity of the objections—the taxes —the wild prairies—the inopportune time—are identical.

It is true that there is always a large class in every community that is never ready to incur the expense of public improvements —that is never willing to pay its share, and opposes everything that costs money. But I am confident that the people of Denver do not contain a very large proportion of such.

READING NO. 13

William Wetmore Story, 1819-1895 [13]

William Wetmore Story, sculptor, essayist, and poet, friend of the Brownings, Henry James, and Charles Eliot Norton, was considered America's outstanding representative of the arts in the 1870's at home and in Europe. He did much to gain acceptance of classical art in the waning period of the picturesque. He is buried in the Protestant Cemetery in Rome under a stone which reads, "IL SIMPATICO AMERICANO."

We as a nation have built our home. It is useful. It is commodious. To its practical departments we have given much thought. But art as yet has no place in it. We claim to be a

[13] William Wetmore Story, "Fine Arts," in *Reports of United States Commissioners Paris Universal Exposition, 1878* (Washington, 1878), pp. 169-170.

practical people. We insist that use is better than beauty; that if our national house is not decorated and beautified, it is because beauty is of no practical benefit to men. We talk perpetually of our being a new country, whose business it is to fell forests, open new paths, plant sawmills, build towns and railways, and attend to business. Undoubtedly this is our duty, but not all our duty, nor the highest and best part of it. A new country, forsooth! As if any people of Anglo-Saxon origin—with all its world of inherited literature behind it and Shakespeare for an ancestor; with all its history stretching back in direct line two thousand years; with all its religion and law derived from the past—could possibly be called young! As if the mere facts of place made a people young! As if we should all be old if we're on European soil, and are only young because we are on American soil! Do we plead ignorance of finance, of war, of trade, of commerce, of mechanics, on that score? Is there any nation that stands more forward than we in these departments? Why, then, should we excuse ourselves for deficiencies in higher culture by such a plea? We know that it is false. We know that it is only an excuse. So far from this being the case, we are one of the most luxurious nations in the world; one of the most developed in all that relates to convenience and the practical requirements of life, one of the most accomplished in all the so-called useful and mechanical arts; but in the ideal spheres of art we have accomplished little, because we have desired little; our needs and necessities have been amply supplied, but the heart and soul have been fed upon husks. Use has its buildings and habitations, but beauty has not yet its temple. . . .

Hunt the Innovator II[14]

To the French-trained Hunt goes the honor of designing the first apartment house in New York, the Stuyvesant, until recently standing at 142 East 18th Street. He is also responsible for organizing the architectural profession in America and for training a whole generation of well-known architects in his studio, just as he himself had trained in the studio of Lefuel in Paris, helping the Emperor's architect to design a new pavilion at the Louvre.

Hunt helped to establish The Architectural Review financially, and his diary records advice given to the editor in 1888 to stress the classic principles that govern architecture, rather than those of the picturesque movement which lead only to shallowness and frivolity.

In his office there were no stereotyped practices and perfunctory methods of work, no servile and convenient copying of features and details from the work of the past; his architecture was not to be a mechanical rehash of what had already been done, but a free and inspired effort, a process of bold thinking and 'true designing' with a conscious artistic purpose. Moreover, architectural designing was to be under determined mental control, not haphazard, not an 'accident' of mere draftsmanship; the pencil was not to run away with set opinions of what would be right and sensible. Moderation was to reign at all times. The general character and cost of a building was to be proportionate to its uses; plain-purpose buildings were to receive plain treatment, the highest resources and effects of the art were to be reserved for the highest tasks. In short, there were to be no shirt-waist factories designed like Paris hotels or Oxford college buildings, no fire-apparatus houses like French castles; there was to be no prostitution of the choicest features of past styles nor

[14] R. M. Hunt, "A Reminiscence and an Appreciation," in *The Architectural Record*, 39 (March, 1916), pp. 295-96, and "Richard M. Hunt, Master Architect and Man," some reminiscences by Frank E. Wallis, in *The Architectural Review*, v. 22 (November, 1917), pp. 239-240.

of the most competent invention by ourselves upon the ordinary, everyday problems of buildings, simply because, perhaps, we could 'afford it.' Mr. Hunt thought, in a higher sense, that we could not at all afford to do this. . . .

And thus, when Mr. Hunt started practice in New York, he applied these ideas as an artistic creed, a conviction, as a 'mission', he hoped, for American architecture. Here in the United States, there seemed indeed a field, he thought, where architectural practice was less rigidly tied down to the tyranny of tradition, school and established taste, and where something might be done in the way of making a fresh and clean start toward better things. Mr. Hunt was favorably situated financially, by connections, by his artistic reputation, by his personal earnestness and eloquence to secure a class of work and clientage that gave him the opportunity to express his faith. As a result there appeared, successively, such buildings as the Tribune Office, the Coal and Iron Exchange, the Victoria Hotel, the Lenox Library, various apartment buildings and work of similar class, variety and design in other cities. These designs constituted an architectural sensation, they were, in fact, a revelation; they were, alike, admired and condemned, praised as works of new inspiration, or denounced as a mere fad and mannerism. . . .

The *Architectural Review* was born at about the same time as our world was awakening to the fact that the art of designing and the trade of building were distinct—if importantly related —functions. This was a distinction for which Hunt had always stood, boldly and unequivocally. It is a standard that, unfortunately, has been lowered in the years that have since elapsed— for the lack of just such a dominating personality to uphold and maintain it until today.

On one occasion, I remember returning to the office, smoking a cigar, on a Saturday afternoon, when the old gentleman caught me playfully, conducted me to his private office, and ordered me to "throw away that damn'd stevadora, take off your coat, and smoke a real cigar." He had the habit of keeping one of the side drawers of his flat-top desk filled full of loose, large, black cigars. Holding me by the shoulder, he rammed the end of one in my mouth, struck a match, and was applying the light to the cigar when George Vanderbilt quietly entered. The old gentleman shouted, "Stay outside, damn it! Stay outside until I get this cigar going. Wallis is so damned particular about his smokes. . . ."

Lawrence, who carried out Biltmore, will remember the old gentleman coming to the office with the entire scheme of that great palace completely laid out on the back of an old envelope; and I think Dick Hunt will recall the scheme for the Administration Building at the Chicago Fair; each laid out in the same manner on an old envelope. I don't believe that any architect, except possibly Wren, or Da Vinci, or Michelangelo, had such a complete control of mass and of a problem as a whole as did Hunt. . . .

When his son Joe sailed for Paris, the chief came in and, hunching himself in his desk chair, sad and lonely, with tears and an absent expression in his eyes, to my question, he replied, "Wallis, my boy Joe is gone, and I may never see him again." Strange to say, he never did see his boy again. I have often thought of his last days in Newport, and his strange cry for a sight of Joe, who could not return in time to see his old Dad. These occurrences showed me the close relationship between his delicate sweetness and his powerful, masterly manhood, and they explain somewhat why his personality so dominated the profession, for I have seen, several years after his death, at a great dinner, when his name was mentioned by the speaker, the entire body of two hundred men on their feet, shouting, "Hunt—Hunt —Hunt!" . . .

READING NO. 15

The Tenement House Death Rate[15]

Before the coming of the dumb-bell tenement (see Reading No. 27), *in itself no great advance, the early waves of speculative multiple housing had produced a nightmare environment which by the 1870's was being linked by social reformers with crime and disease. The slums were considered a menace to so-*

[15] Charles F. Wingate, ed., "Tenement House Regulation" and "A Few Suggestive Facts," in *The Plumber and Sanitary Engineer,* (New York, October, 1878, and October 15, 1880), pp. 229, 263.

ciety, meaning the middle class. This attitude pervades the hous-
ing movement until quite recent times, when the point of view
of the slum resident finds advocates in the highest circles of
government. (See Readings Nos. 42 and 43.)

We are glad to learn that the Metropolitan Board of Health
have determined to rigidly enforce the law in relation to the
sanitary condition of tenement houses, and to refuse permits to
all builders whose plans do not fulfill the necessary requirements
for lighting, ventilation and drainage. When it is considered how
large a proportion of our population occupy tenement houses,
—fully 190,000 families in 66,000 tenements,—and also that
more than half the mortality (65 to 70 per cent.) of the city
occurs in, and is due to the deficiencies of this class of dwellings,
it is vitally important that no pains should be spared to improve
them in every possible way. Hitherto, there has been considerable laxity in regard to this matter. Many architects have not
been aware of the actual features of the law, and the building
department has granted permits in many cases where the statute
was wilfully violated. At one of their late meetings, Mr. Carl
Pfiffer, consulting architect of the Board, reported unfavorably
upon several tenement house plans which had been submitted
to him, and, it was decided to make a test case of several and
to refuse permits until the plans were modified so as to harmonize
with the law. The main difficulty seems to be the lack of proper
extensions of hallways on the upper stories, so as to afford sufficient light and air.

An unfortunate error which crept into the legislature act regu-
lating these buildings, has been taken advantage of by unscrupulous builders. The act directs that no building shall be erected
in the rear of another, unless there is a clear open space between the two buildings of from 10 to 25 feet according to the
height of the structures; but, as this does not forbid the erection
of *a front building* where the rear lot is already occupied, this
loop hole has been used to enable some of the most unsanitary
dwellings in the city to be erected.

A vast improvement has been effected in the condition of
tenements in New York through the efforts of the health authorities. The uprooting and eradication of the notorious Gotham
Court in Cherry street, is a single instance of what has been

accomplished in this direction. The owners of such buildings, influenced by a wholesome fear of incurring public exposure and legal penalties, have greatly improved the sanitary features of many of these dwellings. Yet, much still remains to be accomplished in this direction, in order to satisfy the growing requirements of the public. Not a few of these dwellings are unfitted for human habitation, and should be torn down and removed; others need to be overhauled and thoroughly renovated. It is the duty of the Health Board to carry through these important reforms, and we are confident public opinion will fully sustain it in the undertaking. . . .

Probably 75 per cent. of the maladies of the city, which often pass over into the better quarters, arise from the tenement houses. The death rate of the Fourth, Sixth, and Seventeenth Wards is double that of the up-town wealthy districts. *Ninety per cent.* of the children born in these dens die before reaching youth.

The amount of sickness is proportioned to the death rate. There is a gradual physical degeneracy. Wasting diseases prevail. Infantile life is nipped in the bud; youth is deformed and loathsome; decrepitude comes at thirty. The slow process of decay is aptly called "TENEMENT HOUSE ROT."

The frequent expression of the poor, "We have no sickness, thank God," is uttered by those whose sunken eyes, pale cheeks, and colorless lips, speak more eloquently than words, of the unseen agencies that are sapping the fountains of health.

Religious teachers and philanthropists agree that it is useless to try to improve the moral condition of the tenement-house class until their physical surroundings are reformed.

Their intellects are so blunted, and their perceptions so perverted, by the noxious atmosphere which they breathe, and the all-pervading filth in which they live and move and have their being, that they are not *susceptible to moral and religious* influences.

Bad tenement houses become hot-beds of vice and crime. "Most of the young criminals," says the Prison Association, "come from these dwellings."

The latter created a proletaire class who have no interest in the permanent well-being of the community, who have no sense of home, and who live without any deep root in the soil, the mere tools of demagogues and designing men.

Per contra, wherever there has been a great improvement made in the condition of dwellings for the poor, disorderly and criminal conduct has immediately and greatly diminished.

The overcrowding of New York Population is equalled by no other city in the world. In the Fourth Ward alone there are 290,000 inhabitants to the square mile. In London, the most densely populated districts reach in St. James 144,000, in St. Luke, 151,000, in East London, 175,000 to the square mile. There are *eleven* persons on the average to each house in New York—in Philadelphia only six or seven.

Some 500,000 persons in our city live in tenement houses, and a large portion of these inhabit rooms which are never lighted by the sun in winter, or sleep in bed-rooms which are never aired except from the dwelling room.

To briefly summarize these statements, the existing and crying evils of tenement house life are:

1. *Squalor, discomfort, intemperance, herding like cattle, filth.*

2. *Chronic disease, sweeping epidemics, and decimation by death, THE LITTLE CHILDREN being the victims.*

3. *Family disruption, growth of immorality and vicious habits.*

4. *The creation of and fostering of crime.*

These evils have become chronic. They are accepted as a matter of course by most persons. The terrible consequences which must follow their existence are ignored or forgotten. Yet their continuance is a blot upon our civilization, a criticism upon Christianity. The voice and influence of every good citizen should be freely given to secure their removal. They cannot be suffered to exist any longer.

Birth Pains of the World's
Columbian Exposition[16]

The White City was born in a depression and its effect on Chicago's real estate development, while important in The Loop (see Chapter 4), were less tangible on the South Side. Homer Hoyt's pioneering study undertaken in the 1930's remains the standard work on Chicago's physical growth up to that time.

The World's Fair.—The fact that a World's Fair to celebrate the four-hundredth anniversary of the voyage of Christopher Columbus would probably be held somewhere in the United States in 1892 led to anticipations as early as 1887 that Chicago would be selected as the site. The Chicago members of Congress worked with such astuteness to effect political combinations to bring this about that by 1889 Chicago was considered the probable choice of Congress. Although New York was a serious contender for the honor, with St. Louis and Washington as other candidates, Chicago received the majority vote of Congress on February 25, 1890. This favorable action had already been largely anticipated by local real estate men, but non-resident owners of Chicago property were so surprised that they advanced the prices of their holdings 25 per cent or withdrew them from the market altogether.

After Chicago had been selected as a site, there was a baffling delay of over six months before it was decided in what part of the city the Fair would be held. At first there were proposals for dividing the Fair into two sections, giving part to the South Side and part to the West or North sides. A united Fair was next decided upon, and the first location picked for it was on the lake front near the downtown area on two hundred acres of ground to be made on the lake front for that purpose. In spite of a majority decision in favor of the lake-front site, a minority, led by Lyman J. Gage, influenced partly by the fear that the

[16] Homer Hoyt, *One Hundred Years of Land Values in Chicago*, University of Chicago Press (Chicago, Illinois, 1933), pp. 155-157.

manufacture of so much new land would lower the value of central business property, induced the World's Fair Commission to select Jackson Park as the main site of the Fair. The lake front, however, was to be retained as the gateway to the Fair. West Side politicians then attempted some machinations with the state legislature that would put Jackson Park out of the running. The South Park Commissioners had sought permission to issue bonds to drain Jackson Park, the cost of which was to be borne by the people as part of the permanent expense of improving the park, for it was believed that those promoting the Fair would not incur this cost when other sites already improved were available. Those favoring the West Side parks as a site for the Fair sought to prevent a law authorizing this South Park bond issue from being passed. This indirect attack failed, however, and the West and North sides were eliminated as possibilities. The exact location of the Fair was not yet settled. The idea of extending the Fair along the lake front north of Jackson Park was abandoned and the consent to use the Midway in addition to Jackson Park was obtained from the South Park Commissioners. The request made in September, 1890, for the use of Washington Park also started a wild boom in lots along Cottage Grove Avenue from Forty-ninth to Sixtieth streets, but this movement collapsed when the South Park Commissioners refused permission. After many months of vacillation, the selection of Jackson Park and the Midway as the only site of the Fair was finally made.

The expectation that Jackson Park would be the final choice as the site of the Fair had already caused land values nearby to rise to what the real estate editor of the *Chicago Tribune* called "crack-brained altitudes." The chances of the West and North sides had always seemed so remote that they never had an appreciable land boom on the possibility of securing the Fair. The imagination of the times alternated from speculation about the site of the Fair to the actual content of the Fair itself. Some of the bizarre and grandiose conceptions of projected World's Fair towers may give the readers an idea of the extravagant fancies of a boom era.

The effect of the World's Fair on land values in the vicinity of Jackson Park and the Midway had been almost fully discounted before the end of 1890, nearly three years before the Fair opened its gates. In the meantime, during 1891 and 1892 landowners in that vicinity sought to realize something on their investment in land which they were unable to sell at a profit by building World's Fair hotels and apartments. Many of these were built along Fifty-fifth Street and near Jackson Park. The extravagant hopes that were entertained as to the possible income to be derived from World's Fair guests were doomed to grievous disappointment. The crowds were slow in coming, the full peak of attendance lasted only a short time, and soon after the close of the Fair most of these projects were in the hands of receivers. The low rents at which the vacant apartments were offered in the winter of 1893-94 attracted tenants from all parts of the city to this section. . . .

READINGS NOS. 17 AND 18

Speculation, Urban and Rural

Speculation in land could lead to development or its reverse, a shattered image. There were thousands of paper cities like Nasby's oil boom town, but the Bronx became a reality in the third dimension when Henry Morgenthau and his associates organized the subway boom on land opened up by the transit lines. Morgenthau later became U.S. Ambassador to Turkey and Mexico, and his son was Secretary of the Treasury under Franklin D. Roosevelt.

URBAN [17]

In 1904, as the subway neared completion, I was astonished to find that there had been no activity in real estate in anticipation of the benefits that would accrue from the increased transportation facilities in the upper part of New York and the Bronx. I therefore enlisted the assistance of my nephew, Robert E. Simon, and of J. Clarence Davies, and organized what was dubbed by some of the real estate operators the 'Subway Boom'.

[17] Henry Morgenthau, in collaboration with French Strother, *All in a Life-Time* (New York, Doubleday, 1922), pp. 87-88.

On behalf of the company and some associates, we purchased all the big plots that abutted the various transit lines, and could be secured at reasonable prices. In a period of ninety days we purchased in the Bronx, in the Dyckman district, in Washington Heights, and Fort George, about 2,500 lots which were eventually sold for $9,000,000. . . .

RURAL [18]

The regulation building, for business and dwelling purposes, was a story-and-a-half frame house, gable end to the street, and, as a rule, unpainted. The few that had been painted looked worse than those that had not—healthy, natural ugliness being always preferable to decayed beauty. Besides the honest, weather-beaten walls, the patchy red and white of such as had been painted and peeled looked as though they had an attack of timber-measles, and never got over it. The town had the whole prairie to grow over; and might have reached a hundred miles north and a hundred miles south without barrier; but, as if land was too dear to be wasted, lots were laid out as in the heart of a city, twenty by a hundred feet, giving room enough in front for a patch of red and white balsams, and behind for a clothes-line. The wood-pile was invariably in the back alley, which differed in no respect from the back alleys of other Western villages. A broken wagon stood at the entrance, convenient for the thin and piratical pig to pensively scratch against; its entire length was strewn with oyster and tomato cans, baking-powder tins, and broken dishes, left by the receding waves of the twice-yearly house-cleaning. Its precincts were sacred to that emblem of immortality—the cast-off hoop-skirt, the only article, too good to throw away and too bad to steal, left it in the alley, sure of finding it should it ever be wanted. Wheel-barrows with broken wheels, old bedsteads, chairs mourning legs, burned-out stoves, cupboards that would not fit—everything that, from through carelessness or lack of use, demanded storage-room, was left in the alleys, to the weather, the pigs, and the boys. . . .

New Canton was the moon-ribbed, ill-fed ghost of a city— not a one-horse but a one-mule town, begotten by the lying

[18] D. R. Locke (Petroleum V. Nasby, pseud.), *A Paper City* (Boston, 1879), pp. 11-13.

promise of four spectral railroads, on the expectation of an impossible ship-canal. One speculator, with cheek of brass and tongue hung upon seivel; three speculators not so gifted, but equally unscrupulous, with just as little to lose; and one honest but deluded man, adopted the creature, and chattered men into the belief there was stuff in it for a lusty present and a vigorous future. . . .

READING NO. 19

Hunt the Innovator III[19]

Architects of the classical revival have been called superficial and worse by contemporary critics in their attempts to conceal the deficiencies of Picturesque Secessionism. That Hunt planned his buildings with the client in mind, in this case the visitors to the Chicago World's Fair, is made clear in the following passage which also reveals his mastery of the principles of composition.

By a remarkable piece of fortune, the architects to whom the five buildings on the great court were assigned constituted a family, by reason of long-established personal relations and of unusually close professional sympathies. Of this family Mr. Hunt was the natural head; two of its members, Post and Van Brunt, were his professional children; Howe, Peabody, and Stearns, having been pupils and assistants of the latter, may be considered the grandchildren of the household; while McKim, who had been brought up under the same academical influences, was, with his partners, of the same blood by right of adoption and practice. Collaboration under such circumstances, and under a species of parental discipline so inspiring, so vigorous, and so affectionate, should hardly fail to confer upon the work resulting from it some portion of the delightful harmony which prevailed in their councils.

[19] Henry Van Brunt, "Architecture at the World's Columbian Exposition," *The Century Magazine*, XLIV (1892), pp. 89-94.

By common consent the most monumental of these buildings—that devoted to the Administration—was undertaken by Mr. Hunt. Having all the elements of an academical project of the first class, it was eminently fitting that this important structure should fall into hands so admirably equipped by learning and experience to do it full justice. It was to occupy the western or landward side of the great court, and to stand in its main central axis at the point where this axis was intersected by a transverse axis which ran north and south between the Mines and Electricity buildings. It was designed to be the loftiest and most purely monumental composition in the Park, and to serve not only for the accommodation of the various bureau of administration, but, more conspicuously, as the great porch of the Exposition. The area assigned was a square measuring about 260 feet on each side, and it was necessary to divide it into four equal parts by two great avenues crossing at right angles on the axial lines which we have described. In fact, the building was in some way to stand on four legs astride this crossing of the ways, like one of the quadrilateral Janus-coaches of the Romans, but on a much greater scale. The whole system of railway communication was to be so connected on the west with this building, that the crowds of visitors, on arriving, should enter and cross this ceremonial vestibule; should there obtain their first impressions; and by the majesty and spacious repose of the interior, should be in a manner introduced into a new world, and forced into sympathy with the highest objects of this latest international exposition of arts. Its function, indeed, was that of an overture.

These conditions suggested to Mr. Hunt the idea of a civic temple based upon the model of the domical cathedrals of the Renaissance. Following this type, he projected, upon the crossing of the two axial lines, a hall of octagonal plan; but unlike the cathedrals, this hall was designed to form the fundamental basis, the leading motive, of the design, not only on the interior but on the exterior of the structure, there being neither nave nor transepts to interfere with the clear external development of this dominating feature from the ground to the summit. Thus, at the outset, he secured that expression of unity which is essential to the noblest monumental effect in architecture. The expression of repose, at once majestic and graceful, which is no less essential, was to be obtained, not only by a careful subordination of detail to the leading idea, but by such a disposition of masses as would impart an aspect of absolute stability. This implied the necessity of procuring a pyramidal or culminating effect; the whole com-

Fig. 4. FOCAL POINT OF THE CHICAGO EXPOSITION. *The domed central hall of the World's Fair of 1893 by the New York architect Richard Morris Hunt, called by critics "an object lesson in the potentialities of classic design." (Note the echo of ancient Rome in rostral columns on the bridge over the canal.) (After Talbot F. Hamlin,* The American Spirit in Architecture.*)*

position, from bottom to top, preparing for this effect by some process of diminution by stages upward. To this end he enveloped his hall (which the conditions of area permitted him to make 120 feet in interior diameter) with two octagonal shells about 24 feet apart, the space between being occupied by galleries, elevators, vestibules, and staircases. Against the alternate or diagonal sides of the octagon he erected four pavilions in the form of wings 84 feet square, in four stories, in which he accommodated the various offices of administration; the archways, pierced through the four cardinal sides of the octagon, being externally recessed between these pavilions, thus affording two direct, broad passageways through the building at right angles. These pavilions are so treated as to be in scale with the other buildings of the great court, and are carried to the same height of 60 feet, thus securing four wide-spreading abutments with flat, terraced roofs. Above these the outer octagonal shell of the central mass detaches itself, and asserts its outline against the sky through another stage, where it stops in the form of a gallery, decorated with bronze flambeaux, and permits the inner shell in turn to become outwardly manifest in a third stage of diminished diameter, rising in an octagonal drum, the whole mass finishing with the soaring lines of the central dome; which by vertical growth, determined by conditions of proportion reaches the height of 275 feet from the pavement. Enriched with decorated ribs and sculptured panels, and made splendid with shining gold, this noble dome rises far above the other structures of the Exposition, proclaiming afar the position of its monumental gateway.

But as the inner surface of the outer dome would form a ceiling far too lofty to serve as a proper and effective cover for the hall, it became necessary, in order to give proper proportions to this monumental chamber, to construct an inner and lower dome, 190 feet high from the pavement, with an open eye at the apex, through which from below could be seen the upper structure, like the cope of a mysterious sky beyond. This architectural device is similar to those used by Mansart in the dome of the Invalides at Paris, by Soufflot in the Pantheon, and by Wren in St. Paul's at London, which rank nexet to St. Peter's as the largest and most important of the great Renaissance temples of Europe. It also appears in the rotunda of the national Capitol at Washington. But, as conceived by Hunt, the exterior dome of the vestibule of the Exposition is 42 feet higher than that of Mansart, 45 feet higher than that of Soufflot, about the same height as that of St. Paul's, and 57 feet higher than that of our national Capitol, exclusive of the lantern in each case. The interior dome has a height from the pavement 15 feet higher than that of the Invalides; it has about the same height as that of the French Pantheon; is 20 feet lower than that of St. Paul's, and 10 feet higher than that of the Capitol at Washington. In diameter it surpasses all these domes, being 38 feet wider than the first, 56 feet wider than the second, 12 feet wider than the third, and 26 feet wider than the Washington example. Indeed, in this regard, it is only 20 feet less than that of St. Peter's at Rome, which, however, in exterior height exceeds the American model by 90 feet, and in interior height by 143. Being thus in dimensions inferior only to the work of Michelangelo, it may be considered, in this respect, at least, an adequate vestibule to the Exposition of 1893.

The method of lighting the interior of this vast domical chamber in a proper and adequate manner was a problem so important that Mr. Hunt considered it one of the primary formative influences controlling the evolution of his architectural scheme. One of the noblest effects of interior illumination known in historical art is in the Roman Pantheon, the area of which (140 feet in diameter) is lighted only by the circular hypethral opening 25 feet wide at the apex of the dome, 140 feet from the pavement. Inspired by this majestic example, Mr. Hunt proposed in this respect to depend mainly upon such light as could be obtained from the open eye of his lower dome, 50 feet wide and 190 feet from the pavement, which should in turn borrow its light from the illumination of the space between his outer and inner domes through a glazed hypethral opening 38 feet wide, forming the summit of the building, and taking the place of the lantern or belvedere which usually forms the finial of the greater domes of the Renaissance.

In his decorative treatment of the problem thus evolved Mr. Hunt has exercised a fine spirit of scholarly reserve. The architectural language employed is simple and stately, and the composition as a whole is so free from complications, its structural articulations are so frankly accentuated, that it is easy to read, and, being read, cannot fail to surprise the most unaccustomed mind with a distinct and veritable architectural impression. But to obtain this simplicity of result a far greater knowledge of design and far more ingenuity of adaptation have been required than if the building had been sophisticated with all the consciousness and affectations of modern art. In order to bring his design into the family of which, by the adoption of a common module of proportion, the other buildings of the groups around the great court are members, Mr. Hunt's four pavilions of administration, forming the lower story of the facades, are treated externally, like them, with a single order raised upon a basement. He has preferred the Doric in his case, so as to obtain by contrast with its neighbors an effect of severe dignity and what might be called colossal repose, and to provide for a gradual increase of enrichment in the upper parts of his monument. His second story is Ionic, with an open colonnade, or loggia, on each of the cardinal faces of the octagon, showing the inner shell behind, and with domed circular staircase pavilions of the same order on the narrower alternate sides, niched between heavy corner piers, which bear groups of statuary, thus obtaining a certain degree of movement and complication in the outlines of his design, and enhancing its pyramidal effect. On all his exterior he has used conventional ornament with great reserve, depending for richness of effect upon three colossal groups of statuary on each of his administrative pavilions, upon two, flanking each of his main entrances, and upon eight, crowning the gallery below the drum of his dome.

This sculpture, the work of Mr. Karl Bitter of New York, is characterized by great breadth and dignity of treatment, and by that expression of heroic power and fitness which is derived from knowing how to treat colossal subjects in a colossal way, and how to model figures so that they may assist the main architectural thought and not compete with it. Thus the groups which crown the corner piers of the four wings in the lower part of the building are in repose, and are so massed that they serve properly as monumental finials, while those surmounting the gallery above are more strongly accentuated, so as to become intelligible at that great height, and are distinguished by a far greater animation of outline and lightness of movement, by means of gesture, outspread wings, and accessories, so that they may act as foils to the simple and stately architectural lines of the dome, at the base of which they stand, and so that they may aid it in its upward spring. The subjects are apparently intended to typify, in a succession of groups, beginning in the lower parts of the

monument, the advance of mankind from barbarism to civilization, and the final triumph of the arts of peace and war.

Unlike the other buildings of the Exposition, Mr. Hunt's has
two sets of facades, an exterior and an interior. In the latter he
has not repeated his exterior orders, and the same self-denial
which has chastened and purified the exterior has left these inner
walls large, simple, and spacious, not even the angles of the
inclosing octagon being architecturally emphasized at any point.
Each of the eight sides of this interior octagon is pierced with an
archway occupied by a screen of doors below and bronze grilles
above; over these is a series of panels filled with sculpture and
inscriptions, and upon the great interior cornice which crowns
these walls is a balcony, like the whispering-gallery of St.
Paul's, by means of which the scene may be viewed from above.
An order of pilasters directly under the inner dome surmounts
this gallery, and the dome itself is decorated with panels, the
whole interior being enriched with color, so disposed as to
complete and perfect the design.

We have already said that this vestibule was intended to introduce the visitors to the Exposition into a new world. As
they emerge from its east archway and enter the court, they
must, if possible, receive a memorable impression of architectural
harmony on a vast scale. To this end the forum, basilicas, and
baths of the Roman Empire, the villas and gardens of the princes
of the Italian Renaissance, the royal courtyards of the palaces of
France and Spain, must yield to the architects, "in that new
world which is the old," their rich inheritance of ordered
beauty, to make possible the creation of a bright picture of
civic splendor such as this great function of modern civilization
would seem to require.

At the outset it was considered of the first importance that
the people, in circulating around the court and entering or leaving the buildings, should so far as possible be protected from
the heat of the midsummer sun. To assist in accomplishing this
object the great quadrangle will be closed in by a series of
sheltered ambulatories, like the Greek stoa, included in and
forming a part of the facades of the palaces of Machinery and
Agriculture on the right, and of the Liberal Arts and Electricity
on the left. The vast fronts of these buildings, far exceeding in
dimensions those of any other ancient or modern architectural

group, with their monumental colonnaded pavilions, their
sculptured enrichments, their statuary, domes, and towers, will
appear in mellowed ivory marble, relieved by decorations in
color in the shadowy recesses of the porticos. Immediately
before him the stranger will behold the great basin 350 feet
wide and 1100 feet long, stretching eastward in the middle of
the court, bordered with double walled terraces, of which the
lower will be decorated with shrubbery and flowers, and the
upper, with balustrades, rostral columns, vases, and statuary.
Broad stairs descend from the main porticos of the buildings to
the water, and the canals, which enter the basin on each side,
are crossed by monumental bridges. On the nearer margin of
the greater basin, and in the axis of the court, he will see a
smaller circular basin 150 feet in diameter, on a level with the
upper terrace, flanked by two lofty columns bearing eagles.
In the center of this, on an antique galley of bronze 60 feet
long, eight colossal rowers, portraying the Arts and Sciences,
stand, four on a side, bending to their long sweeps; in the prow
is poised the herald Fame, with trump and outspread wings;
while aft, Time, the pilot, leans upon his helm; and, high aloft
on a throne, supported by cherubs, Columbia sits, a fair, youth-
ful figure, eager and alert, not reposing upon the past, but poised
in high expectation. Eight couriers precede the barge, mounted
upon marine horses ramping out of the water. The whole triumphal pageant is seen through a mist of interlacing fountain-
jets, and from the brimming basin the water falls 14 feet in a
series of steps into the greater sheet below, a half-circle of
dolphins spouting over the cascade. This pompous allegory is the
work of the sculptor Frederick MacMonnies. At the outer end
of the basin a colossus of the Republic, by the sculptor Daniel
C. French, rises from the water. It is treated somewhat in the
Greek archaic manner, with a strong accentuation of vertical
lines, but with a simplicity and breadth which give to the figure
an aspect of majesty and power. Beyond it, a double open
colonnade, or peristyle, 60 feet high, like that of Bernini in
front of St. Peter's, forming three sides of a square, closes in
the great court toward the lake. Of the two wings of this colonnade one is a concert-hall, and the other a casino or waiting-hall
for passengers by boat. Its columns typify the States of the
Union. In the center of this architectural screen is a triumphal

arch thrown over the canal which connects the basin with the harbor. Through this and through the open screen of the colonnade one may see the wide-spreading lake, the watery horizon, and, still in the axis of the court and a thousand feet from the shore, a lofty pharos with an island-casino at its base. Animating the whole, banners and gonfalons flutter gaily from innumerable staffs; people of all nations walk in the shadow of the porches, linger on the bridges, crowd along the broad pavement of the terraces, and watch from the balustrades the incessant movement of many-colored boats and electric barges upon the water. . . .

READING NO. 20

What Architecture Is "American"?[20]

In the first quarter of the twentieth century arose an American architecture which influenced the art all over the world. Talbot Hamlin was its earliest historian, but its contributions have yet to be properly evaluated by contemporary critics.

But the new American Renaissance was characterized by a new psychology of style. Style became no longer an idol, as in the strict revival days. Historical style was aid only, a means, to be used as the designer wished, freely or strictly. The character of the basic design—planning, expression, composition—that was the big, the deciding element. . . .

The new Renaissance was characterized by a new honesty and a new joy in the use of materials. Colors and textures began to be played against each other, made an integral part of the design. Terra cotta, *faïence,* glass mosaics, rough bricks, roof tiles, metal work—all were used, experimented with. Often an exaggerated, restless richness was the result, particularly in exterior work; yet the tendency served to set the artist free, to widen his field and broaden popular appreciation.

[20] From The Pageant of America Series. Copyright Yale University Press. United States Publishers Association, Inc., sole distributors.

And one other underlying tendency ran through the period; a tendency that has its roots back in the years immediately following the War of Independence—a tendency towards the increasing use of classic forms. All through the Civil War the United States capitol dome had been growing—and the influence of that never stopped. All through the time of the Gothic Revival, of the artistic bathos of the 'sixties and 'seventies, some type of classic had seemed the accepted, the natural style for such monumental buildings as state capitols. And with the coming of the new Renaissance with its growing sense of restraint and dignity, its growing mastery of an eclectic classicism, this innate and natural love for classic forms could not but be enlarged. In the choice of a classic style for the World's Columbian Exhibition in 1892-93 the consulting architects only symbolized popular taste; in the actual creation of the tremendously impressive group of buildings with their ranked arches and columns they did more; they astonished, delighted, and fixed popular taste. The Chicago World's Fair was climactic as the Centennial at Philadelphia was epoch-making; one ushered in a period of gestation and growth; the other was the symbol of the arrival at full birth of that which may be called modern American architecture. . . .

READINGS NOS. 21 AND 22

Private Enterprise and Public Control[21]

Railroad and company towns continued to be built throughout the first decades of the twentieth century, the former dwindling in numbers and the latter gaining. (See Chapter 5.) In contrast to the laissez-faire attitudes which pervaded new town building, an early measure to restrict the height of buildings near the

[21] William A. Bell, M. A., M. B., Cantab., *New Tracks in North America*—"A Journal of Travel and Adventure whilst engaged in the survey for a southern railroad to the Pacific Ocean during 1867-1868" Horn & Wallace (Albuquerque, New Mexico, 1965), pp. 17-19.

*Capitol is referred to in Burnham's letter. The Chicago planner
was then building Washington's Union Station, a forerunner of
the great termini which were celebrated in the prose of Thomas
Wolfe and other contemporaries.*

Wholesale town-making may not be a romantic theme, or one
capable of being made very attractive to the general reader; but
it is the great characteristic of this part of our route, and is
only to be seen to perfection along the line of these great railways. On the Platte, where the central line across the continent
often advances at the rate of two miles a day, town-making is
reduced to a system. The depot at the end of the line is only
moved every two or three months; and as rich valleys are far
scarcer in this section of country than in Kansas, the town
usually moves also, while nothing remains to mark the spot
where thousands lived, but a station, a name, and a few acres
of bare earth. Last winter, Cheyenne was the terminal depot on
this route, and increased in size to 5,000 inhabitants. A man I
met at Denver, who had just come from Cheyenne, told me that
while he was standing on the railway platform, a long freight
train arrived, laden with frame houses, boards, furniture, palings,
old tents, and all the rubbish which makes up one of these mush-
room "cities." The guard jumped off his van, and seeing some
friends on the platform, called out with a flourish, "Gentlemen,
here's Julesburg." The next train probably brought some other
"city," to lose for ever its identity in the great Cheyenne.

The men of Kansas have discovered in these towns as fine
a field for speculative amusement as the best managed Homburg
could offer. Thousands of dollars are daily won and lost all along
the line by speculating in town lots. A spot is chosen in advance
of the line, and is marked off into streets, blocks, and town lots,
sometimes by the railway company, sometimes by an independent land company. As the rails approach it, the fun begins,
and up goes the price of the lots, higher and higher. At last
it becomes the terminal depot—the starting-point for the western
trade—where the goods are transferred from the freight vans
to the ox trains, and sent off to Denver, to Santa Fe, Fort
Union, and other points. It then presents a scene of great activity,
and quickly rises to the zenith of its glory. Town lots are bought
up on all sides to build accommodation for the traders, teamsters,

camp-followers, and "loafers," who seem to drop from the skies. This state of things, however, lasts only for a time. The terminal depot must soon be moved forward, and the little colony will be left to its own resources. If the district has good natural advantages, it will remain; if not, it will disappear, and the town lots will fall to nothing. . . .

[*On January 22, 1902, Burnham wrote to McKim:*]

D. H. B. to McKim[22]

DEAR CHARLES: The display in Washington was beyond my expectations, and although I realized that it would be impressive I was unprepared for its effect on me. I congratulate you on the success of your work. It is greater than I dared hope for. The only disappointment arose from Curtis's model of the Mall as it is proposed to be. Its unfinished condition is responsible for this. He could in a day bring it up and I hope he has done so ere now. . . . I notice you have made the plaza in front of the station a half-circle. I should have liked this and so drew it at first, but it is impracticable, and no other form out of fifty tried meets the requirements as does the one sent the Engineer Commissioner. . . . After another fit of fear and trembling I asked Mr. Cassatt to let me lower the depot twenty-odd feet. It was in the bill prepared by the engineers +66, the Capitol being only about +86. This made me fear the competition of the two structures. Mr. Cassatt not only agreed, but gave us praise for a more sensible railway solution. I think we may get it down to nearly +40. We are nearly there now.

Ely said that you and he felt that I am doing too much for my work and myself. All I know is that I am doing better work than I did in the years that are gone, and that I do my work easier.

[22] Letter from Daniel Hudson Burnham to McKim, January 22, 1902, in Charles Moore, *The Senate Park Commission* (Boston and New York, 1921), v. 1, p. 168.

The Later Utopias

Communism and Christian Socialism produced late nineteenth-century utopias, of which Bellamy's was the most famous. His book Looking Backward *was a best-seller for many years. When William Dean Howells embraced Tolstoyan socialism, his novelist's eye brought out the ills of American society as strongly as the exquisite pleasures of Altruria, which he set outside the United States. Among the many utopian colonies started in California, one took the name and Howells' inspiration; the venture was started by a Unitarian minister, Edward Biron Payne, in 1894. Stressing interdependence and mutual obligation among men, Altruria's life, like all similar experiments outside the mainstream, was brief, but not, as Ambrose Bierce suggested, entirely "a ludicrous fizzle."*

By WILLIAM DEAN HOWELLS, 1894 [23]

". . . But won't you explain to me first something about your deserted farms here? It's quite a new thing to me."

"It isn't a new thing to us," said the young fellow, with a short laugh. "And there isn't much to explain about it. You'll see them all through New England. When a man finds he can't get his funeral expenses out of the land, he don't feel like staying to be buried in it, and he pulls up and goes."

"But people used to get their living expenses here," I suggested. "Why can't they now?"

"Well, they didn't use to have western prices to fight with; and then the land wasn't wornout so, and the taxes were not so heavy. How would you like to pay twenty to thirty dollars on the thousand, and assessed up to the last notch, in the city?"

"Why, what in the world makes your taxes so heavy?"

"Schools and roads. We've got to have schools, and you city folks want good roads when you come here in the summer, don't you? Then the season is short and sometimes we can't make a crop. The frost catches the corn in the field, and you have your

[23] W. D. Howells, *A Traveler from Altruria* (New York, 1894), pp. 138-141.

trouble for your pains. Potatoes are the only thing we can count on, except grass, and when everybody raises potatoes, you know where the price goes."

"Oh, but now, Mr. Camp," said Mrs. Makely, leaning over towards him, and speaking in a cosy and coaxing tone, as if he must not really keep the truth from an old friend like her, "isn't it a good deal because the farmers' daughters want pianos, and the farmers' sons want buggies? I heard Professor Lumen saying, the other day, that if the farmers were willing to work, as they used to work, they could still get a good living off their farms, and that they gave up their places because they were too lazy, in many cases, to farm them properly."

"He'd better not let *me* hear him saying that," said the young fellow, while a hot flush passed over his face. He added, bitterly, "If he wants to see how easy it is to make a living up here, he can take this place and try, for a year or two; he can get it cheap. But I guess he wouldn't want it the year round; he'd only want it a few months in the summer, when he could enjoy the sightliness of it, and see me working over there on my farm, while he smoked on his front porch." He turned round and looked at the old house, in silence a moment. Then, as he went on, his voice lost its angry ring. "The folks here bought this place from the Indians, and they'd been here more than two hundred years. Do you think they left it because they were too lazy to run it, or couldn't get pianos or buggies out of it, or were such fools as not to know whether they were well off? It was their *home;* they were born, and lived and died here. There is the family burying ground, over there."

Neither Mrs. Makely nor myself was ready with a reply, and we left the word with the Altrurian, who suggested, "Still, I suppose they will be more prosperous in the west, on the new land they take up?"

The young fellow leaned his arms on the wheel by which he stood. "What do you mean by taking up new land?"

"Why, out of the public domain"—

"There *ain't* any public domain that's worth having. All the good land is in the hands of railroads, and farm syndicates, and speculators; and if you want a farm in the west you've got to buy it; the east is the only place where folks give them away, because they ain't worth keeping. If you haven't got the ready money, you can buy one on credit, and pay ten twenty and thirty per cent. interest, and live in a dugout on the plains— till your mortgage matures." The young man took his arms from the wheel and moved a few steps backward, as he added, "I'll see you over at the house later."

By WILLIAM DEAN HOWELLS, 1907 [24]

I despair of giving you any *real* notion of the capitals, but if you remember the White City at the Columbian Fair at Chicago in 1893, you can have some idea of the general effect of one; only there is nothing heterogeneous in their beauty. There is one classic rule in the architecture, but each of the different architects may characterize an edifice from himself, just as different authors writing the same language characterize it by the diction natural to him. There are suggestions of the capitals in some of our cities, and if you remember Commonwealth Avenue in Boston, you can imagine something like the union of street and garden which every street of them is. The trolleys run under the overarching trees between the lawns, flanked by gravelled footpaths between flower-beds, and you take the cars or not as you like. As there is no hurry, they go about as fast as English trams, and the danger from them is practically reduced to nothing by the crossings dipping under them at the street corners. The centre of the capital is approached by colonnades, which at night bear groups of great bulbous lamps, and by day flutter with the Altrurian and Regionic flags. Around this centre are the stores and restaurants and theatres, and galleries and libraries, with arcades over the sidewalks, like those in Bologna; sometimes the arcades are in two stories, as they are in Chester. People are constantly coming and going in an easy way during the afternoon, though in the morning the streets are rather deserted.

But what is the use? I could go on describing and describing, and never get in half the differences from American cities, with their hideous uproar, and their mud in the wet, and their clouds of swirling dust in the wind. But there is one feature which I must mention, because you can fancy it from the fond dream of a great national highway which some of our architects pro-

[24] W. D. Howells, *Through the Eye of the Needle* (New York and London, 1907), pp. 184-186.

jected while they were still in the fervor of excitement from
the beauty of the Peristyle, and other features of the White
City. They really have such a highway here, crossing the whole
Altrurian continent, and uniting the circle of the Regionic capitals. As we travelled for a long time by the country roads on
the beds of the old railways, I had no idea of this magnificent
avenue, till one day my husband suddenly ran our van into the
one leading up to the first capital we were to visit. Then I
found myself between miles and miles of stately white pillars, rising and sinking as the road found its natural levels, and growing
in the perspective before us and dwindling behind us. I could
not keep out of my mind a colonnade of palm-trees, only the
fronds were lacking, and there were never palms so beautiful.
Each pillar was inscribed with the name of some Altrurian who
had done something for his country, written some beautiful poem
or story, or history, made some scientific discovery, composed
an opera, invented a universal convenience, performed a wonderful cure, or been a delightful singer, or orator, or gardener,
or farmer. Not one soldier, general or admiral, among them!
That seemed very strange to me, and I asked Aristides how it
was. Like everything else in Altruria, it was very simple; there
had been no war for so long that there were no famous soldiers
to commemorate. . . .

READINGS NOS. 25 AND 26

Return to Splendor: 1903-1905

*Augustus St. Gaudens, Karl Bitter, and other sculptors had
been active in the Chicago World's Fair of 1893; and the former
advised on the replanning of the Mall in Washington. Later,
when Picturesque Secessionism rose again, architects and sculptors were to go their separate ways; but in the City Beautiful
period they saw the value of teamwork. They also saw the
importance of working to a plan in which individual buildings
and monuments were sometimes subdued for the good of the
whole, an attitude which has completely vanished from modern
architecture and design.*

Reading No. 26 is from an address by Theodore Roosevelt.

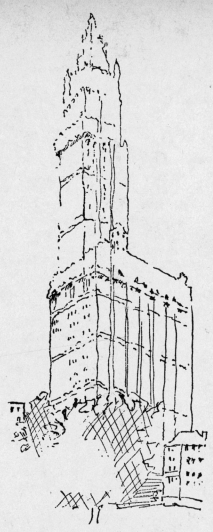

Fig. 5. THE TOWER-FORM SKY-SCRAPER. *The Woolworth Building by Cass Gilbert (constructed 1911-13), then the tallest building in the world. The surface is a decorative terra-cotta, employed at all levels. The horizontal lines show an early use of service mezzanines housing the mechanical equipment.*

By AUGUSTUS ST. GAUDENS [25]

August 15, 1903.

My dear Mr. President:

. . . I have been very apprehensive with regard to the disposition of the new Public Buildings proposed in Washington. It would be deplorable in the extreme if they were not placed according to some comprehensive plan, binding all the Public Buildings with some idea of unity and harmony. Even if the scheme suggested by the commission of which I was a member, was discarded, I cannot express too strongly the hope that nothing will be done without first consulting professional men, not directly interested in any one building. . . .

AUGUSTUS ST. GAUDENS

By THEODORE ROOSEVELT [26]

. . . All that it means is that whenever hereafter a public building is provided for and erected, it should be erected in accordance with a carefully thought-out plan adopted long before, and that it should be not only beautiful in itself, but fitting in its relations to the whole scheme of the public buildings, the parks and the drives of the District.

Working through municipal improvement commissions, very great progress has already been made in rendering more beautiful our cities from New York to San Francisco. An incredible amount remains to be done. But a beginning has been made and now I most earnestly hope that in the national capital a better beginning will be made than anywhere else; and that can be made only by utilizing to the fullest degree the thought and the disinterested efforts of the architects, the artists, the men of art, who stand foremost in their professions here in the United States, and who ask no other reward save the reward of feeling that they have done their full part to make as beautiful as it should be the capital city of the Great Republic.

[25] Personal letter from Augustus Saint-Gaudens to the President, August 15, 1903, in *The Reminiscences of Augustus Saint-Gaudens* (New York, 1913), p. 272.

[26] Addresses at the Annual Dinner of the American Institute of Architects, 1905, in *The Promise of American Architecture* (Washington, 1905), p. 18.

Coping with the Slum Problem

In 1877 Henry C. Meyer, a public utilities manufacturer, founded The Plumber and Sanitary Engineer. *In a competition run by this journal, the dumb-bell tenement, designed by James E. Ware, won the prize. The Tenement House Law of 1879, requiring every bedroom to have a window but doing little to reduce congestion on the 25 by 100 foot lot, ensured the spread of the dumb-bell apartment all over New York between 1879 and 1901.*

After 1890 Jacob Riis, a friend of Theodore Roosevelt, publicized the idea of model tenements combined with restrictive legislation. He described the problems of the poor at the turn of the century in vivid prose and revealing photographs, discovering at the same time many of the hidden traditions of slum life.

By HENRY C. MEYER [27]

During this same summer of 1884 a Royal Commission was in session taking evidence on the problem of the "Housing of the Working Classes." William T. Stead's book the "Bitter Cry of Outcast London" having aroused a strong public interest.

I was invited by the commission to give evidence—this I did on July 4th, 1884—this was published in their final report, and which, I now reproduce in this appendix. . . .

14,043. (*The Chairman.*) You are editor and proprietor of the "Sanitary Engineer" in New York, are you not?—I am.

14,044. The condition of the New York tenement houses before 1879 was extremely bad, was it not?—It was.

14,045. What were the greatest difficulties which you met with in attempting to secure remedial legislation before that time?—We had about 21,000 tenement houses and about 18,000

[27] Henry C. Meyer, "Minutes of Evidence—July 4, 1884" from *The Story of the Sanitary Engineer* (later *The Engineering Record*) supplementary to *Civil War Experiences* (New York, 1928), pp. 31, 33-34, 36-37.

owners; certain of them managed to maintain what we call in America a "lobby" at the legislature, to defeat any attempt on the part of the health authorities to secure control of the erection and maintenance of such buildings.

14,046. There was a great agitation which resulted in the passing of the Tenement House Act in the year 1879, was there not?—There was.

14,047. What powers were conferred by that Act?—Prior to the passage of that Act about 90 per cent. of the city lot could be covered. The authorities could not well reach old dwellings that were built for other purposes, and that were subsequently converted into tenement houses; such buildings always had a large proportion of dark inside rooms. The division of land in our city is very unfortunate, the blocks being 400 ft. long by 200 ft. deep; the streets are 60 ft. wide, and 90 per cent. of each 100-ft. lot could be covered. The buildings were usually put up five stories high, and the landlords generally tried to provide for four families on a floor. You can imagine in our climate, from June, from May indeed, till the last of September, the condition of the occupants of the large majority of the inside rooms with, for two months, the thermometer averaging over 80. Our infant mortality of course ran up directly in these hot months. The tenement houses were also in many instances owned by people of no great means, and they felt that it would ruin them, if they had to do this, or that, or the other thing, in the matter of improvements. At any rate the board of health in trying to get powers had been thwarted. . . .

14,050. (*Mr. Jesse Collings*.) By "covering the lot," do you mean to what extent the lot should be covered by houses, and what proportion should be left as an open space?—Yes. I have brought one or two drawings with me from the Health Exhibition to give you an idea. That is the shape of a New York lot (producing a plan). There is another lot like this at the back of it. They are built right up, and the block is 400 feet long. Builders used to cover nearly the whole lot, with a dark stairway on the side. They never employed an architect, as a rule, to build a tenement house, it was just a stereotyped pattern. The idea was to get as many rooms as possible in the building, and allow as small a space for the stairway as practicable. Under the new law the Board of Health were given absolute discretion as to how the 65 per cent. should be utilized. Sometimes the location of the lot made it undesirable to leave all the vacant space upon the rear, or to make into a court; and the board has absolute discretion to approve of the plan which, in their judgment, best met the conditions laid down by the law. This was one of the modifications of one of the prize plans (producing another plan). It is what we call the dumb-bell plan. If a house is built on either side you get a large court in the centre. The Board of Health have also absolute control over the drainage. The builder is obliged to file his plan to show how much vacant space he intends to leave, the size of the transoms over the door, and the size of the windows; and if it is approved an inspector is detailed to watch the work, because builders do not always carry out the work in accordance with the plans. . . .

By JACOB RIIS [28]

The community has asserted its right to destroy tenements that destroy life, and for that cause, we bought the slum off in the Mulberry Bend at its own figure. On the rear tenements we set the price, and set it low. It was a long step. Bottle Alley is gone, and Bandits' Roost. Bone Alley, Thieves' Alley, and Kerosene Row—they are all gone. Hell's Kitchen and Poverty Gap have acquired standards of decency; Poverty Gap has risen even to the height of neckties. The time is fresh in my recollection when a different kind of necktie was its pride; when the boy murderer—he was barely nineteen—who wore it on the gallows took leave of the captain of detectives with the cheerful invitation to "come over to the wake. They will have a high old time." And the event fully redeemed the promise. The whole Gap turned out to do the dead bully honor. I have not heard from the Gap, and hardly from Hell's Kitchen, in five years. The last news from the Kitchen was when the thin wedge of a column of negroes, in their uptown migration, tried to squeeze in, and provoked a race war; but that in fairness should not be laid up against it. In certain local aspects it might be accounted a sacred duty; as much so as to get drunk and provoke

[28] Jacob A. Riis, *A Ten Years' War; An Account of the Battle with the Slum in New York* (Boston and New York, 1900), pp. 19-20.

a fight on the anniversary of the battle of the Boyne. But on the whole the Kitchen has grown orderly. The gang rarely beats a policeman nowadays, and it has not killed one in a long while. . . .

READINGS NOS. 29 AND 30

Charles Mulford Robinson:
Reports on Honolulu (1906)
and San Jose, California (1909)

Charles Mulford Robinson was a propagandist of the City Beautiful. As a planner, he lacked the grand concepts of a Burnham or a McKim, but his books were popular. Until World War I he received many commissions from civic improvement societies and local governments. The following excerpts from two of his little-known reports reveal his general approach, which may be compared with that of his younger contemporary, the "practical" John Nolen. (See Chapter 5.)

HONOLULU [29]

To the Honorable The Board of Supervisors, County of Oahu, Hawaii Territory.

Gentlemen: In accordance with your request, I have examined the city of Honolulu and its immediately tributary country, with a view to making recommendations and suggestions for its improvement. I understand that in making recommendations which may be called practicable, I am not restricted to the immediately possible, but am asked to lay down a plan for the county to work toward in the years to come. The idea, I take it, is to accomplish at once so much as may be, making

[29] Charles Mulford Robinson, *The Improvement of Honolulu* (March 14, 1906), pp. 1-3.

sure the while that each step, however little, counts in the right direction, toward the realization of a complete and systematic scheme.

The word "improvement" I do not interpret as meaning an attempt to enhance the extraordinary natural beauty that has been spread around you, but the increase of its accessibility and the silencing of jarring notes. My errand is not to "paint the lily"—that cannot successfully be done; but, rather, to facilitate the enjoyment of it. For this reason, I find the special emphasis in my report appearing very naturally on parks and drives. But before coming to specific recommendations, there are certain general considerations that I desire to call to your attention and that are to be regarded as a part of the report.

Among these I might fittingly, and pleasantly, include a discussion of the future of Honolulu, as the playground of the well-to-do and the popular stopping point for the tourist travel that is to flow in growing volume across the Pacific. This, however, seems to have been pretty fully done by others; and it is much more necessary for you to take thought of the means by which you will command such good fortune, through proving worthy of it, than to expend your time and mine in prophecy as to what will happen if you do make yourselves so attractive that no one will want to pass you by without a visit and that many will come to see these islands only. In these considerations, also, the appeal is to commercial motives. It should be higher. When all is said, whatever development is given to Honolulu and to its surrounding country, should be first of all for the comfort and the pleasure in life of its own citizens. They pay the bills, they live—instead of visiting—here, and in suggesting improvements for Honolulu we have to consider what will improve it for them, make it better worth living in, add to the comfort and the pleasure in life of its own citizens. If we make the city more beautiful to them, adding to their contentment and happiness, we shall also make it more attractive to strangers. For a town is not like a picture, simply to be looked at and admired; it is to be lived in, and loved; and the more lovable it is the more people will come to it.

The lovable quality is personality. The home is attractive, however modest its cost, that expresses personality. So the town, which is the home of many, must have an individuality in keeping with its citizens, and must express it, if it is to please them

and to attract others. And towns do have individuality. There
never have been two cities just alike, and he would be a ruth-
less iconoclast who would try to pattern one city after another.
We must preserve the individuality of Honolulu, or its charm
will depart. Cut through broad avenues and boulevards, build
a hot and sunny quay, widen your streets and straighten them,
spend enough money in such measures hopelessly to bankrupt
the city, and when the work is all done the winsomeness of
Honolulu will have departed, and it will always be spoken of
as the town that was spoiled. So my first charge is, be true
to yourselves. Do not dream of what other cities may have done;
but, far isolated from them, develop your own individuality, be
Hawaiian, be a more beautiful Honolulu. Then you will have
distinction, and only then. . . .

SAN JOSE [30]

But my own preference is not adopt fixed rules for the pro-
portioning of roadway, parking and sidewalk on streets of given
width. Each street should be considered, I believe, on its merits.
It cannot be said that every street of forty feet has a certain
amount of vehicular traffic, and every street of fifty feet a certain
other amount; and unless we can say that, it were idle to allot
a certain width of roadway to every street in each group. One
street may be arterial, and carry a heavy through travel from
the country, or from some nearby town, in addition to its normal
local traffic. Another street may be so interrupted by parks or
other obstructions as to carry no through travel and quickly to
lose its local travel. Or, again, the closeness of the building on
a street, or the number of semi-public structures it contains—
such as churches, or halls, or railroad stations,—calling many people to them, influence the volume of the travel. We do not make
all the rooms of a house the same size, nor do we say that
every room of a given size must have a certain amount of
window space and door space. We adapt the room to its purpose,
and so each street in a city should be planned with a view to
the part it is to play, and should be given just as wide a parking
as the traffic will properly permit. In San Jose this will almost
always be more than the ordinance—which, being general, is

[30] Charles Mulford Robinson, *The Beautifying of San Jose; A Report
to the Outdoor Art League* (California, January, 1909), pp. 11-12.

necessarily conservative,—now allows. Merely to take down the fences and widen the side parking will do much to make San Jose more beautiful.

READING NO. 31

The Zoning Power[31]

In the 1920's zoning quickly became a field for experts, city planners especially being required to testify on the innumerable cases that arose as a result of its rise in popularity. The following excerpt from a book by a well-known Harvard planner of the day gives a typical illustration of the way in which this exercise of the police power was regarded in his circle.

Telephone companies have been generous in reporting economies already effected in their work through zoning, and undoubtedly before long we may have some figures from fire insurance companies as to the reduction in the fire risk effected through the greater yard requirements usually prescribed in zoning ordinances. Although fire prevention campaigns are responsible for some of the savings in Grand Rapids, Mich., it is noticeable that fire losses in Grand Rapids have been reduced from $7.76 per capita in 1923 (the year in which zoning was passed) to $1.73 in 1927, and some of this saving was reported as attributable to zoning.

Whatever effects in terms of dollars and cents may be directly attributed to zoning, the greatest and most desirable effect has been a social one, in the protection of home life and the stimulation of home neighborhoods. The examples are too numerous to specify: there was scarcely a zoned community visited which

[31] Theodora Kimball Hubbard and Henry Vincent Hubbard, *Our Cities Today and Tomorrow; A Survey of Planning and Zoning Progress in the United States,* Harvard University Press (Cambridge, 1929), p. 191.

did not report the feeling of protection and security prevailing in home neighborhoods, and frequently the stimulation of a distinctly better type of residential development. "What Zoning has Done for the City of Providence," issued by the Board of Review in 1928, is an encouraging record of the results of well administered zoning. The decreased density of population in residential areas effected by zoning cannot fail to have a marked favorable effect, as noted in Memphis, where there is a distinct feeling that accidents to children have been reduced through the segregation of uses effected by zoning. In Newton, Mass., zoning is accounted the vital factor in producing a rapidly growing city of homes. The creation of a desirable residential area has been particularly well illustrated in St. Paul in the Highland Park section: when the $10,000,000 Ford plant was located there, zoning helped to make the necessary adjustments and to stop speculation in store sites which was already beginning to threaten areas appropriate for home neighborhoods. In Washington, D.C., zoning has undoubtedly stimulated a demand for neighborhoods of detached homes, and, as already proved, this has been kept strongly in view during recent studies for zoning revisions.

Although this social result achieved in the improvement of home and community life is so intangible, it is after all the end-product of stabilized property values and the ultimate justification of zoning as an exercise of community control over private rights in the interest of health, safety, morals, and the general welfare.

The Neighborhood Unit[32]

The Regional Plan of New York, instigated by Charles Dyer Norton, the Chicagoan who, as president of the Commercial Club, had hired Burnham and Bennett to draw up the plan of Chicago, contained Clarence Perry's prescription for the school-centered neighborhood, which was later attacked by intellectuals in the planning profession either for its fostering of "a child-centered world," as they termed it, or for its abuse by certain groups as a means of obtaining racial exclusiveness.

It is with the neighborhood itself, and not its relation to the city at large, that this study is concerned. If it is to be treated as an organic entity, then it logically follows that the first step in the conversion of unimproved acreage for residential purposes will be its division into unit areas, each one of which is suitable for a single neighborhood community. The next step consists in the planning of each unit so that adequate provision is made for the efficient operation of the four main neighborhood functions. The attainment of this major objective—as well as the securing of safety to pedestrians and the laying of the structural foundation for quality in environment—depends, according to our investigations, upon the observance of the following requirements:

Neighborhood-Unit Principles

1. Size.—A residential unit development should provide housing for that population for which one elementary school is ordinarily required, its actual area depending upon population density.

2. Boundaries.—The unit should be bounded on all sides by arterial streets, sufficiently wide to facilitate its by-passing by all through traffic.

[32] Clarence Arthur Perry, *The Neighborhood Unit* in *Neighborhood and Community Planning* by the Committee on Regional Plan of New York and its Environs (New York, 1929), pp. 34-35.

3. Open Spaces.—A system of small parks and recreation spaces, planned to meet the needs of the particular neighborhood, should be provided.

4. Institution Sites.—Sites for the school and other institutions having service spheres coinciding with the limits of the unit should be suitably grouped about a central point, or common.

5. Local Shops.—One or more shopping districts, adequate for the population to be served, should be laid out in the circumference of the unit, preferably at traffic junctions and adjacent to similar districts of adjoining neighborhoods.

6. Internal Street System.—The unit should be provided with a special street system, each highway being proportioned to its probable traffic load, and the street net as a whole being designed to facilitate circulation within the unit and to discourage its use by through traffic.

READING NO. 33

The Metropolitan "T"[33]

The sprawling city of Los Angeles, for years the butt of jokes in magazines like Variety, *which has been wont to refer to it as "the unscrambled egg" or "seven freeways in search of a city," appears to be developing a mammonth center ("colossal" is a more frequently used term thereabouts), which may indeed turn out to be the central place for all the counties of Southern California.* (See Chapter 6.) *The following promotional piece, written in enthusiastic Los Angelese, could be as prophetic as any current regional science research, and is probably as accurate.* (*Note the reference to Manhattan in the mention of the Wilshire corridor and also the acceptance of a rapid-transit future.*)

[33] "The Metropolitan "T" " in *Los Angeles Magazine,* 11, January, 1966, pp. 29-30.

Now, finally and unmistakably, some 185 years after its founding and yet a mere 65 years since graduating as the population leader of its class, this formless Angel among cities is beginning to take recognizable form. The population pressure continues, but now there is a sense of shape and structure, as well as cultural substance, to the city.

The long sought-after high density, high rise metropolitan center for Los Angeles and, indeed, all of Southern California is emerging in the shape of a "T," whose slanting top-bar angles from the Music Center southeast to the renewed USC campus. This top-bar, five miles long, encompasses the civic center, Dodger Stadium, the soon-to-be-built convention center, the old but fast revitalizing commercial core, the Sports Arena and Coliseum.

The T's upright, of course, is the 15-mile Wilshire corridor, a corridor about the same length and width as Manhattan, running west to the ocean, high-rising and handsome.

In its functional relationship to the surrounding suburbs, the Metropolitan T can be expressed as in "Town"—downtown, midtown and uptown. Other major commercial and service clusters, such as Hollywood and the airport complex, once separate and distinctive "communities," are increasingly regarded as districts, and they too are oriented towards the Metropolitan T.

Freeways outline the T. To the south of Wilshire is the Santa Monica Freeway, spinning off the circle of downtown interchanges and stretching in virtually a straight line to the sea. A parallel freeway a short distance to the north of Wilshire, the Beverly Hills Freeway, is now in the final planning stage. But the real sense of direction for the city and easy mobility for the Metropolitan T will come with the construction of a subway, across downtown then out (and under) Wilshire.

The consensus is that rapid transit for Los Angeles—a prototype system unique to this new form of decentralized megapolitan area, combining a metro subway with above-ground trains reaching into the suburbs—will become a reality within the decade. The financing go-ahead signal, which must be given at the polls, is still almost two years away . . . but anticipating the obvious, major structures rising along Wilshire are already incorporating subway entries and exits.

The list of stops one might presently make along Wilshire is imposing in its variety and length: the new "Wilshire Center" hotel and Tishman building complex . . . the Art Museum . . . the "Miracle Mile" . . . The Beverly Hills triangle of smart shops . . . the big, always-active UCLA campus . . . Century City (soon to add a theater to stage new productions after a brief Broadway try-out) . . . reawakened Santa Monica, with a new shopping mall and complementing high rise . . . the Beach.

Downtown, in addition to its Bunker Hill development and relatively-new Occidental Tower, has its first 40- and 42-story buildings going up—the Union Bank-Connecticut Life Insurance building at 5th & Figueroa and the Crocker-Citizens Bank building at 6th & Grand. At least eight new high rise structures for Wilshire Boulevard are in the works. But, surely, the biggest and perhaps the best are yet to come, and soon.

It is, thus, reasonable to expect that this midtown section now largely occupied by Fremont Place and, ironically, before that by the pioneer mansion of "Crazy Jack" Barnett, will in time be the site of the Metropolitan T's tallest structures. Perhaps, following the trend set by Chicago, the skyscrapers erected there will combine business and institutional offices (with parking spaces) on the first levels, and luxury apartments with patios and barbecues on the upper levels, meshing once and for all the tempo of city life with some of the aloof seclusion and pleasures of the suburbs.

The "what-ifs" in Los Angeles history are without number. What if Los Angeles had been encumbered with the costly high-rise clutter equivalent to that of Fifth Avenue, economically unfeasible to replace? In general, what if it had made mistakes that could not be rectified?

But the pertinence is that, because of still relatively open areas along Wilshire and previous toe-dragging delay in creating a pattern and a master plan for the city, it is possible for Los Angeles to virtually start from scratch, instructed by the past, moving towards what might be called creative evolution. Only now, after only a little longer than half a century of cityhood, are the more permanent commitments being made, and a final city form taking shape.

State Planning[34]

As Governor of New York State, Franklin Delano Roosevelt set out to ameliorate the plight of the farmers, who had entered a long period of depression after 1922. State planning was one of his innovations, giving him valuable experience when the time came to set up the Tennessee Valley Authority.

. . . Hitherto, we have spoken of two types of living and only two—urban and rural. I believe we can look forward to three rather than two types in the future, for there is a definite place or an intermediate type between the urban and the rural, namely, a rural-industrial group.

I can best illustrate the beginnings of the working out of the problem by reviewing briefly what has been begun in the State of New York during the past three years toward planning for a better use of our agricultural, industrial and human resources. . . .

First, the State developed additional State aid for rural education, especially in the communities which are so sparsely settled that one-room schools predominate. This State aid gave the smaller rural schools the same advantages already enjoyed by the schools in the larger communities.

Second, a fair equalization of State aid to towns for the maintenance of dirt roads was accomplished by putting it on the basis of mileage rather than of assessed valuation.

Third, through a gasoline tax, additional aid was given to the counties for the development of a definite system of farm-to-market roads.

Fourth, the State embarked on a definite program of securing cheaper electricity for the agricultural communities. It proposes to harness the St. Lawrence River as part of this program, and the electricity developed is by the new law intended primarily for the farmer, the household user, and the small industrialist or storekeeper rather than for large industrial plants.

This was the program to relieve immediate needs. . . .

As a nation we have only begun to scratch the surface along these lines and the possibility of diversifying our industrial life by sending a fair proportion of it into the rural districts. Cheap electric power, good roads and automobiles make such a rural-industrial development possible. Without question there are many industries which can succeed just as well, if not better, by bringing them to rural communities. At the same time these communities will be given higher annual income capacity. We will be restoring the balance.

Through such state planning as I have just outlined many of the problems of transportation, of over-crowded cities, of high cost of living, of better health for the race, of a better balance for the population as a whole, can be solved by the states themselves during the coming generation. . . .

READING NO. 35

Recognition of the Need for National Planning[35]

The initial report on cities made by the Urbanism Committee of Harold Ickes' National Resources Committee in 1937 called for a nationally-organized system of urban reporting and research, something which is still lacking in our knowledge of urban affairs. The urban sociologist Louis Wirth was a member of the committee, which suggested also that "a more decentralized metropolitan pattern would loosen up the areas of congestion," then as now an argument used by the Decentrists in favor of dispersal of industry, offices, and homes away from the old centers.

[35] U.S. Natural Resources Committee, *Our Cities; Their Role in the National Economy* (Washington, 1937), p. 35.

The redistribution of the urban population into the peripheries of metropolitan regions involves the close and constant dependence of the suburban communities upon the economic and technical functions and cultural opportunities which the metropolis provides. The model suburb, whether it is industrial or residential, however superior, aloof, and detached it may believe itself to be, has its basis of existence and draws much of its sustenance from the noisy, grimy city of which economically and culturally it is an integral part, but from which it has managed to remain independent politically.

It has been said that the suburbanite shuttles back and forth from a place where he would rather not live to a place where he would rather not work. In his daily or periodical pendular movement, of which the clock and the time schedule are symbolic, the suburban commuter exhibits the peculiar segmentalization between working and living so characteristic of modern urban society. The bedrooms of American cities are increasingly to be found in the dormitory colonies of the suburbs. The suburbanite, who in his daily routine oscillates between his vocation involving the humdrum, high-speed, technical work of business, industry, and the professions in the heart of the metropolis, and his avocation, which may range from amateur gardening and similar pastoral activities to suburban politics, is not an exception to the urban type of personality but is merely a variety of it. The motives leading to this type of existence are to be sought in the urge to escape the obnoxious aspects of urban life without at the same time losing access to its economic and cultural advantages. In the process, the form and the functions of the city are being revolutionized.

Civic Art and Adornment

In the 1930's relief for the unemployed for the first time included artists and architects and often took the form of the decoration of post offices and other public buildings. The painter George Biddle helped to initiate the program, among the administrators of which was Edward Bruce, the corporation-lawyer-turned-painter, whose philosophy on civic art (Reading No. 37) is expressed in the foreword to a book of illustrations on the project. Many years before, the painter, William Morris Hunt, had expressed a similar view (Reading No. 36) while working on his famous mural "Flight of the Night" in the State Capitol in Albany, New York, a sketch of which can be seen in the Boston Museum of Fine Arts.

By WILLIAM MORRIS HUNT [36]

What a big thing a great building is. Think of the crowd of varied interests that are represented in this room. Think of all those men and their families, thinking and working, year in and year out, all to one end—the making of this Capitol. People grumble and whine about the money which is thrown away upon it; but I tell you that it is an immense work, and worthy of any State or nation. It is the greatest thing which this State has ever done, and a very sensible way to spend money. Do you think that it is throwing away money to keep fifteen hundred skilled workmen in one place, and doing one thing? No, sir, it is a good investment, and the more it is done, the richer we shall be. It ought to go on forever. I never felt before what a power the united efforts of hundreds has upon the mind. Just think of being a part of it. Here I am in my own world, and I want to stay here.

[36] Martha A. S. Shannon, *Boston Days of William Morris Hunt* Marshall Jones Co. (Boston, 1923), p. 145.
[37] Edward Bruce and Forbes Watson, *Art in Federal Buildings,* Vol. I, "Mural Designs, 1934-1936" (Washington, D.C., 1936), p. xii.

By EDWARD BRUCE [37]

Up to the time when the Government entered the field of art, painters and sculptors had found it necessary to concentrate in the great financial centers. Roughly speaking, men who were not known in New York, Chicago, San Francisco, or some other great city, found it almost impossible to make a living. The former speculative relationship between the public and the artist made the life of the painter and sculptor a gamble. The star system prevailed in painting and sculpture, if not as obviously at least as effectively as in the case of musicians and actors.

One of the first steps taken by the Treasury Department Art Projects was to initiate a series of competitions which artists could enter anonymously. Indeed they were obliged to enter them anonymously. Mural designs, sculpture models, all were submitted unsigned. The name of the entrant was not disclosed until after the award was made. This method of course was a powerful blow at the star system. For the first time America purchased art on a large scale regardless of the fame of the artists, the purchasing being based entirely on the quality of the work. . . .

. . . As a painter I can't help envying the younger artists who are lucky enough to be growing up under a system of art promotion which has such healthy similarities to the periods in which some of the greatest art in the world was produced. We have found that great art has developed under various conditions, but rarely did the best appear unless the community was back of it. Once more the community is behind the artist. My inference, I hope, is sufficiently obvious. . . .

. . . My pleasure in this work has been to realize once more the value of the artists to their country. Given the opportunity to work in, with, and for, their communities, how well our artists have taken advantage of their unprecedented chances to give their best. Disinterested administration, together with the realization that the civilization of a country reaches its highest development through an encouraged freedom of expression, justify faith. My faith is that as long as the artists of this country can utilize their best powers, without materialistic or petty hindrance, progress, in the highest sense of the word, is our inevitable destiny.

Escape to the Suburbs[38]

Echoing Le Corbusier's slogan of "Soleil-Espace-Verdure", wealthy Upper Bohemians, as Russell Lynes has described them, helped to establish the fashion for modern architecture by building their houses in the woods of New Canaan, Connecticut, or the fields of Bucks County, Pennsylvania. Frank Lloyd Wright outdid all the other architects by siting his famous Kaufmann residence over a waterfall, thus achieving an enviable marriage of building and nature. This escape from the city to an air-conditioned "wilderness" was treated quite solemnly by the press and the architectural magazines; satirical comments like the following still remain quite rare.

ART BELONGS IN THE MODERN HOME!

Enchantingly sleek and simple in appearance—a long white box perched on stilts—the Panther's house is situated in a grove of wonderfully natural looking trees. Mrs. Panther—"Babs" to her many friends in the World Federalists and on the Community Forum Committee—meets us at the door. She is wearing black velvet toreador tights, ballet slippers and a divine yellow linen shirt. With her blonde hair in a horse-tail she looks for all the world like a little girl. "This is my year-round costume," she explains later; "I never wear anything different. You see, the house is temperatrolled."

We glance, fascinated, into the enormous living room—or, as the Panthers call it, the play space. We are speechless with delight: one entire wall is occupied by a vast window (of Sanilite glass, of course, which lets in only the health-giving rays) reaching fifteen feet from brick floor to ceiling. Outside is

[38] Ajax, "Living Outdoors with Mrs. Panther," in *Landscape* (Spring, 1954), pp. 24-25.

Fig. 6. NEW FORMS IN THE LANDSCAPE. The world's first cloverleaf interchange, built in 1928 at Woodbridge, New Jersey, on land which was then largely agricultural. The region is now densely urbanized. (From a photograph, N.J. State Highway Department.)

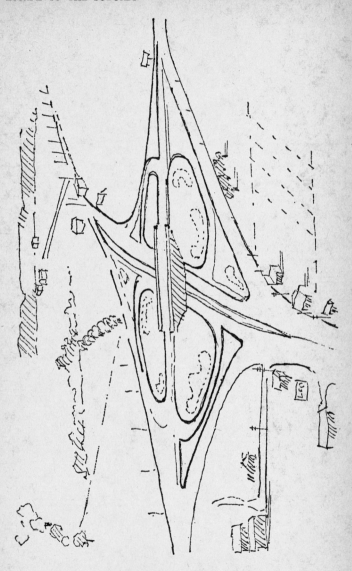

a charmingly unspoilt view of trees and rocks and underbrush. "Here we sit, like Hansl and Gretl, Jeff and I, right in the heart of the woods! We even have a tree here in the middle of the play space!" And so they have: the slender trunk of a maple rises out of the floor and then disappears through the ceiling. "We love our tree," she says softly, laying her hand on the trunk. "The texture of the bark is so exciting. Mies Van Der Rohe was a lamb and let us have it." And how wonderfully *right* it is! It lends just that simple sophisticated touch to the decor of the room. The natural form is repeated by a small but important piece of Henry Moore sculpture on the floor; a witty Calder mobile twinkles overhead. "Don't you adore our tiny little art collection? These two," Mrs. Panther says, "and a sweet little Bracque are all we could afford; we saved and saved and SAVED to buy them." A gay little smile admits us to her confidence. "But we simply HAD to have them," she continues, "because if you love plants and animals and birds the way Jeff and I do you just have to have that kind of art—like nature." . . .

SCIENCE PLUS AMUSING INFORMALITY IS THE WATCHWORD

The Panthers do not sleep or eat out of doors. "Jeff, poor darling, is allergic to practically everything that grows in Connecticut—or anywhere else, for that matter. He has to have an air-conditioned room all of his own." As for eating outside: "Well," Mrs. Panther says with a delightful smile, "I think I prefer to keep the outdoors for the very simplest kind of pleasure. And I adore my work area"—(kitchen in old fashioned parlance) "and spend a great deal of time there. When we have company I open some cans and toss a salad; we have a bottle of French wine, some cheese, and then sit around on cushions and discuss McCarthyism and how we dislike it. I've become quite a cook," she adds proudly. . . .

Yes, we reflect, as Mrs. Panther leads us back into the house, this typical American family leads a *natural* life for young Moderns. The artificialities of city existence are far, far removed from the quiet little eight-room house out there on stilts in the Connecticut woods. Nightclubs, traffic jams, dirt and confusion are no part of their life. Excitement? A casual little concert on recorders, or a new wine and challot sauce Babs discovers, or waking up on a winter's morning to see the Japanese-printlike effect of snow on the black branches—these comprise the Panthers' happiest moments. The Panthers, by the way, have an automatic snowmelting system from garage door to the road a hundred yards distant, so that Jeff need not shovel snow like his Victorian forebears. What's more, it disposes of the melted snow so that no ice is ever formed on the driveway. "Let it snow," says Babs in the words of the once popular song. She turns up the thermostat, adjusts the temperatroll to suit her toreador tights and yellow shirt and little girl hairdo; and once the children have been called for by the school bus she settles down with a volume of her favorite author, André Gide, to enjoy a winter's day in the country. "I'm afraid," she laughingly tells us, "that I wouldn't know how to behave in the city any more. But we young moderns are like that: we want to live abundantly, the way Jeff and I do: in a simple kind of house with this immediate kind of experience of Nature." She thoughtfully caresses the Henry Moore composition. "Or do you think I'm utterly barbaric?"

Well frankly, Mrs. Panther, since you ask. . . .

READING NO. 39

The Coming of Urban Redevelopment[39]

The Housing Act of 1949, in the enactment of which Senator Robert Taft was vitally concerned, set the stage for federally-aided redevelopment of the cities. As the Declaration of Policy makes clear, the primary intention was to redevelop blighted residential areas. Later, with the advent of urban renewal, cities used federal funds to aid in the rebuilding of their downtown commercial centers as well, usually relying on private developers to handle the reconstruction.

[39] Gilman G. Udell, *Home Owner's Loan Acts and Housing Acts* (Washington, 1966), pp. 283-284.

Public Law 171-81st Congress—Declaration
of National Housing Policy

Sec. 2. The Congress hereby declares that the general welfare
and security of the Nation and the health and living standards of
its people require housing production and related community
development sufficient to remedy the serious housing shortage,
the elimination of sub-standard and other inadequate housing
through the clearance of slums and blighted areas, and the
realization as soon as feasible of the goal of a decent home and
a suitable living environment for every American family, thus
contributing to the development and redevelopment of communities and to the advancement of the growth, wealth, and
security of the Nation. The Congress further declares that such
production is necessary to enable the housing industry to make
its full contribution toward an economy of maximum employment, production, and purchasing power. The policy to be
followed in attaining the national housing objective hereby
established shall be: (1) private enterprise shall be encouraged
to serve as large a part of the total need as it can; (2) governmental assistance shall be utilized where feasible to enable private
enterprise to serve more of the total need; (3) appropriate local
public bodies shall be encouraged and assisted to undertake positive programs of encouraging and assisting the development of
well-planned, integrated residential neighborhoods, the development and redevelopment of communities, and the production,
at lower costs, of housing of sound standards of design, construction, livability, and size for adequate family life; (4)
governmental assistance to eliminate substandard and other
inadequate housing through the clearance of slums and blighted
areas, to facilitate community development and redevelopment,
and to provide adequate housing for urban and rural nonfarm
families with incomes so low that they are not being decently
housed in new or existing housing shall be extended to those
localities which estimate their own needs and demonstrate that
these needs are not being met through reliance solely upon
private enterprise, and without such aid; and (5) governmental
assistance for decent, safe, and sanitary farm dwellings and
related facilities shall be extended where the farm owner demon-
strates that he lacks sufficient resources to provide such housing
on his own account and is unable to secure necessary credit for

such housing from other sources on terms and conditions which he could reasonably be expected to fulfill. The Housing and Home Finance Agency and its constituent agencies, and any other departments or agencies of the Federal Government having powers, functions or duties with respect to housing, shall exercise their powers, functions, and duties under this or any other law, consistently with the national housing policy declared by this Act and in such manner as will facilitate sustained progress in attaining the national housing objective hereby established, and in such manner as will encourage and assist (1) the production of housing of sound standards of design, construction, livability, and size for adequate family life; (2) the reduction of the costs of housing without sacrifice of such sound standards; (3) the use of new designs, materials, techniques, and methods in residential construction, the use of standardized dimensions and methods of assembly of home-building materials and equipment, and the increase of efficiency in residential construction and maintenance; (4) the development of well-planned, integrated, residential neighborhoods and the development and redevelopment of communities; and (5) the stabilization of the housing industry at a high annual volume of residential construction.

READING NO. 40

The City as Part of
the National Patrimony[40]

Although the preservation movement in the United States had its origins at the same time as the modern city, notably in the purchase and protection of Mount Vernon by a group of ladies during the Civil War, it is only recently that attention has been paid to preserving whole districts of cities, starting with the

[40] Report of the Conference on Principles and Guidelines for Historic Preservation, Williamsburg, March 1967. Section V. Restoration Principles—C. Area Preservation. (Draft)

Vieux Carré in New Orleans and the Historic District of Charleston, South Carolina, both in the 1930's. The following excerpt illustrates the continuing attempt to set up guidelines in the new field of area preservation, in this case working toward national standards to be used by federal agencies after the passage of the National Historic Preservation Act by the 89th Congress.

Areas to be preserved are those which may include entire rural or urban communities, whose general overall character has either architectural, historical, cultural or aesthetic merit appropriate to an important era or eras. The area might include some diverse elements and need not exhibit only one character, period or flavor nor have any single structure of special significance.

Within historic areas, major elements of town plans should be preserved, including major street patterns, focal elements, public squares, landscaping, vistas, etc. The streetscape, particularly, should be given special attention including consideration of height, rhythm of facades, sight lines, materials, scale, etc.

Very particular attention should be given in those cases where a new element is to be inserted in a substantially complete environment.

Efforts should be made to insure protection of the character of the area by introducing usages which will be of advantage to the community and yet will not require services which would be destructive to the character of the area.

Other areas, not predominantly occupied by structures may include village greens and commons, city squares, parks, geographic features, etc., related to the settlement pattern.

All special areas should be maintained and preserved and guarded from destructive intrusions, and incompatible uses. For the protection and enhancement of such areas, attentions should be given to establishing controls over adjacent properties by easements, zoning, or other means.

Hopes and Fears for the Future

The presidential message on the cities of 1963 should be read in conjunction with the hearings held three years later on the federal role in urban affairs. The testimony given by Congressman Adam Clayton Powell provides reinforcement to the widely-held view that the problems of the modern American city will not be solved until the semi-colonial status of its Negro residents is removed.

By LYNDON B. JOHNSON [41]

To the Congress of the United States:

Throughout man's history, the city has been at the center of civilization. It is at the center of our own society.

Over 70 percent of our population—135 million Americans —live in urban areas. A half century from now 320 million of our 400 million Americans will live in such areas. And our largest cities will receive the greatest impact of growth. . . .

In our time, two giant and dangerous forces are converging on our cities: the forces of growth and of decay.

Between today and the year 2000, more than 80 percent of our population increase will occur in urban areas. During the next 15 years, 30 million people will be added to our cities—equivalent to the combined population of New York, Chicago, Los Angeles, Philadelphia, Detroit, and Baltimore. Each year, in the coming generation, we will add the equivalent of 15 cities of 200,000 each.

[41] President Lyndon B. Johnson in "Message from the President of the United States, March 2, 1965" in the reports of the 89th Congress, 1st session, House of Representatives, Document No. 99, in *Problems and Future of the Central City and its Suburbs*, pp. 1-2.

Already old cities are tending to combine into huge clusters. The strip of land from southern New Hampshire to northern Virginia contains 21 percent of America's population in 1.8 percent of its area. Along the west coast, the Great Lakes, and the Gulf of Mexico, other urban giants are merging and growing.

Our new city dwellers will need homes and schools and public services. By 1975 we will need over 2 million new homes a year. We will need schools for 10 million additional children, welfare and health facilities for 5 million more people over the age of 60, transportation facilities for the daily movement of 200 million people and more than 80 million automobiles.

In the remainder of this century—in less than 40 years—urban population will double, city land will double, and we will have to build in our cities as much as all that we have built since the first colonist arrived on these shores. It is as if we had 40 years to rebuild the entire urban United States.

Yet these new overwhelming pressures are being visited upon cities already in distress. We have over 9 million homes, most of them in cities, which are run down or deteriorating; over 4 million do not have running water or even plumbing. Many of our central cities are in need of major surgery to overcome decay. New suburban sprawl reaches out into the countryside, as the process of urbanization consumes a million acres a year. The old, the poor, the discriminated against are increasingly concentrated in central city ghettos; while others move to the suburbs leaving the central city to battle against immense odds.

Physical decay, from obsolescent schools to polluted water and air, helps breed social decay. It casts a pall of ugliness and despair on the spirits of the people. And this is reflected in rising crime rates, school dropouts, delinquency, and social disorganization.

By ADAM CLAYTON POWELL[42]

The Two Revolutions

During the latter half of that century of the black man's degradation—1910-1960—America witnessed two overlapping major revolutions: the transition from a predominantly rural to urban culture and the accompanying upsurge in migration of black people to the cities.

America has yet to come to grips with the "sturm und drang" of urbanization. As rapidly as we have solved some of the old problems in urban renewal, transportation, education, and fiscal management, employment, industrial development and law enforcement, we have spawned new problems in housing segregation, inferior all-black schools, rising welfare costs, increasing unemployment among black people and police brutality.

Of greater concern to many Americans has been the frightening prospect—for them—of the change from white to black in our cities.

Today, of the 10 largest cities in America, eight have 25% or more black people in their populations. The nation's capital has a majority of black people—63%—while Detroit has 39% black people, Baltimore, 41% black people and Cleveland 34% black people. Across the River from New York City, America's 30th largest city, Newark, is now 40% black.

That the South is not escaping the black migration to the cities is evidenced by the fact that New Orleans is now 41% black, Memphis is 38% black and Atlanta is 38% black. . . .

I would now like to propose the establishment of a National Multi-Purpose Council. The idea for NMPC comes from Dr. Laurence Foster, a former Professor and now Economic Consultant in New York City.

The primary goal of NMPC is the development democratically of a self-directed self-help program for the involvement of residents of urban slums in the redevelopment of these areas through non-profit organizations. A key role for residents of

---

[42] Testimony of Representative Adam Clayton Powell, Chairman, House Education and Labor Committee, before Senator Ribicoff's Senate Subcommittee on Executive Reorganization, in the 89th Congress, 2nd session, August 31-September 1, 1966 (Part 6) (Washington, 1967), pp. 1211, 1213-1215.

slum areas in the *planning, policy making* and *administration* of all redevelopment programs for such areas, as well as in projects to improve human resources would be established.

As a matter of *National Public Policy,* labor, management and government would join together and establish a two-fold program for the renewal of slum areas, namely, the involvement of the residents of the area in the actual job of rehabilitation and new construction by providing residents with: (1) adequate vocational training, and (2) a priority on rehabilitation and construction jobs.

The Urban Renewal Administration of HUD presently requires that funds for urban renewal be granted only to public bodies and agencies. Because of the lack of imagination and respect for human values as evidenced by the Urban Renewal Administration, NMPC would make non-profit corporations eligible for renewal funds and projects. 221(d) (3) permits private, non-profit corporations to build housing. NMPC proposals would broaden their participation in the area of urban renewal.

Specifically, for the NMPC, $35 billion would be appropriated for urban rehabilitation for the next ten years, starting with the black ghettoes of Watts, Chicago's West side, Harlem, Cleveland's Hough and other areas where the black uncared-for live. To insure that such funds would be used to give priority to the poor, funds would be allocated per Congressional District on the basis of median family incomes.

For example, my Congressional District, the 18th, which is substantially Harlem, has a median family income of only $3,999 —the lowest in New York State and 370th lowest of all Congressional districts in America. What a tragic and ironic juxtaposition of living conditions that the 17th Congressional District which is "just across the tracks" from mine has the fourth highest median family income, $8,649, of all Congressional Districts. . . .

I think we can afford to do no less than we are now doing around the world for other people to raise black Americans within the next ten years to the identical economic, educational and political levels of the white Americans.

The problem of second-class citizenship of the black man is not the black man's problem nor is it the white man's problem.

It is not the President's problem, nor is it the Congress' problem. It is an American problem which can only be solved by the collective energies and good will of all Americans. . . .

"And as a single leaf turns not yellow but with the silent knowledge of the whole tree,

So the wrong-doer cannot do wrong without the hidden will of you all."

Further Reading

Charles Abrams, *The City is the Future*. New York, 1965.

Wayne Andrews, *Battle for Chicago*. New York, 1946.

Lewis Alexander, *The Northeastern United States*. Princeton, 1957.

Loren Baritz, *City on a Hill*. New York, 1964.

Alan Burnham, ed., *New York Landmarks*. Middletown, Conn., 1963.

Coles and Reed, *Architecture in America: A Battle of Styles*. New York, 1961.

Collins and Collins, *Camillo Sitte and the Birth of Modern City Planning*. New York, 1965.

Carl W. Condit, *The Chicago School of Architecture*. Chicago, 1964.

Charles N. Glaab, *The American City: A Documentary History*. Homewood, Ill., 1963.

Constance McL. Green, *The Rise of Urban America*. New York, 1965.

Talbot F. Hamlin, *The American Spirit in Architecture*. New Haven, 1926.

Robert V. Hine, *California's Utopian Colonies*. New Haven, 1953.

Charles B. Hosmer, Jr., *Presence of the Past*. New York, 1965.

Jane Jacobs, *The Death and Life of Great American Cities*. New York, 1961.

Roy Lubove, *Community Planning in the 1920's*. Pittsburgh, 1964.

Roy Lubove, *The Progressives and the Slums*. Pittsburgh, 1962.

Charles A. Madison, *Critics and Crusaders*. New York, 1947.

Lewis Mumford, *Sticks and Stones*. New York, 2nd rev. edition, 1955.

Lewis Mumford, *The City in History*. New York, 1961.

John W. Reps, *The Making of Urban America*. Princeton, 1965.

Henry H. Reed, Jr. *The Golden City*. New York, 1959.

Reed and Duckworth, *Central Park*. New York, 1967.

Arthur M. Schlesinger, *Paths to the Present*. Boston, 1963.

Christopher Tunnard, *The City of Man*. New York, 1953.

Tunnard and Reed, *American Skyline*. New York, 1955.

Tunnard and Pushkarev, *Man-Made America*. New Haven, 1963.

Raymond Vernon, *The Myth and Reality of Our Urban Problems*. Cambridge, Mass., 1966.

Richard C. Wade, *The Urban Frontier*. Cambridge, Mass., 1959.

Robert A. Walker, *The Planning Function in Urban Government*. 2nd. edition, Chicago, 1950.

Max Weber, *The City,* trs. and ed. Martindale and Neuwirth. New York, 1962.

Louis Wirth, *On Cities and Social Life*. Albert J. Reiss, ed., Chicago, 1964.

Other reference works are noted in the text. Among the quarterlies and journals, *Journal of the American Institute of Planners, Journal of the Society of Architectural Historians, Landscape, Historic Preservation, Land Economics, Traffic Quarterly, Urban Land* and *Urban Affairs Quarterly* are especially recommended.

Index